Glimpses of Fayetteville's Past

by

Denele Campbell

Articles contained in this work are expanded and revised from articles by the author originally published by the Washington County Historical Society in their quarterly publication "Flashback."

"The History of 546 West Center/541 West Meadow, Fayetteville" was published in the Fall 2007 edition, Vol. 57, No. 4

"Fayetteville Junction: Hub of Washington County's 1885-1935 Timber Boom" was published Winter 2005 edition, Vol. 55, No. 1

"Quicktown: A Relic of Early Fayetteville" was published in the Autumn 2006 edition, Vol. 56, No. 4

"Alcohol Regulation in Early Washington County" was published in the Spring 2009 edition, Vol. 59, No. 1

"Fayetteville's Grocery Stores: 1830-2005" was published in the Summer 2005 edition, Vol. 55, No. 3

Glimpses of Fayetteville's Past

Copyright © 2014 Denele Campbell

All Rights Reserved

Revised Second Edition © 2021 Denele Campbell

All Rights Reserved

Cover Images from 1908 Platbook of Washington

Washington County Website

https://www.co.washington.ar.us/government/departments-a-e/archives/1908-plat-book-of-washington-county

My sincere thanks to all those who strive to document the path of our footsteps. Without the treasury of county archives, newspaper stories, local museums, libraries, and other collections, none of these works would have been possible.

Other Books by Denele Campbell

Notes of a Piano Tuner

Recipes of Trailside Café and Tea Room

I Met a Goat on the Road and other stories of life on this hill

Aquarian Revolution: 32 Interviews, Back to the Land

A Crime Unfit to be Named: The Prosecution of John William Campbell

Glimpses of Fayetteville's Past

Rex Perkins: A Biography

South County: Bunyard Road and the Personal Adventures of Denny Luke

Ray: One Man's Life

Murder in the County: 50 True Stories of Old Washington County

The Violent End of the Gilliland Boys

Self-Publishing: The Basics

The West Fork Valley: Environs and Settlement before 1900

Adventures in Real Estate: A Ridiculous and Mostly Rewarding Journey from Tenant to Landlord

Good Times: A History of Night Spots and Live Music in Fayetteville, Arkansas

Gas, Grass, and Ass: Adventures in Rural America, 1973

A Pitts Family History: A Survey of English Ancestral Origins, Colonial Connections, and Proven Descendants

Table of Contents

The History of 546 West Center Street, Fayetteville 7
The History of Fayette Junction 24
    Fayette Junction 26
    The Railroad Comes to Fayetteville 28
    The Men and Mills at Fayette Junction 33
    Charlesworth Hardwood Lumber Company 34
    W. N. Jones 35
    Sandford Hardwood Lumber Company 36
    Pitkin & Mayes 37
    Sligo Wagon Wood Company 43
    Sligo's Alexander McCartney 46
    Brower Veneer Mill 53
    E. A. Budd 54
    End of the Line 56
    Wye Operations 62
    Tom Hargis 63
    Lumber Warehousing Returns to Sligo Mill Building 68
    Sources for History of Fayette Junction 72
Quicktown: Here then gone 74
The Rise and Fall of Alcohol Prohibition 87
    Regulation of Alcohol in the 1830s 90
    The 1840s 95
    The 1850s 102
    The 1860s and War 112
    The 1870s 117

  The 1880s 122

  The 1890s 128

  A New Century 130

  The Rise in Crime 137

175 Years of Groceries 141

Appendix I: Wagon Production in Fayetteville 178

Appendix II: Sligo 181

Appendix III: The Phipps/Fulbright Mill and Arkansas Forests
.... 187

The History of 546 West Center Street, Fayetteville

The oddly-shaped Quonset hut facing Center Street five blocks west of the Fayetteville Square has been part of the city's landscape since the early 1940s. "Quonset" is a trademark name for a prefabricated structure with semi-circular arched roof of corrugated metal, developed for American military use during World War II. (British engineers had developed an earlier version during World War I.) The Center Street Quonset, built along a spur railroad track as warehouse space, is cut off vertically along its east side so that trains could pass close by for ease of loading. Such an abbreviated version is referred to as a "half-Quonset."

South facade of Quonset 2011. Deck on the right side covers area where railroad tracks once lay.

The Quonset at this location is only the most recent structure to occupy this property. A review of all the enterprise and structures which existed on this half block over Fayetteville's early years provides a fascinating glimpse into the town's progress and the people who made it happen.

When Fayetteville was laid out following a land grant by President Andrew Jackson in 1835, Gregg Street formed the western boundary of Block 21 and of the 160-acre "Original Town." Since swamps and a large creek ran north and south several yards west of Gregg, this was a logical western terminus for the early village. The Quonset sits at the northeast corner of the intersection of Center and Gregg Streets at the south end of a block-long strip of land from Meadow Street to Center, with Gregg Street along the western perimeter. This location was literally the very edge of town.

The first deed record found for this parcel is dated March 14, 1861, in which Roderick M. Webber, his wife Martha, William C. Stout and his wife Mary, and John W. Stout sold land as part of a larger parcel to John B. Chesher for $150. The next record found is dated 1885, three years after the railroad had opened the main track a block west and on the other side of the creek.

Planners deemed the Quonset property part of a suitable route for a spur track that would connect the industrial areas of Dickson and West streets with the industrial and stockyard areas several blocks south between Prairie Street (earlier named "Bridge") and the national cemetery three blocks further south. Surveyed to be one hundred feet wide, with fifty feet either side of the track's centerline, the spur track land was not taken by imminent domain, perhaps because such adverse possessions were legal only for a thoroughfare route.

The railroad purchased acreage from three separate property owners to secure this section of right of way. On May 19, 1885, Preston Johnson sold a strip of land 62 feet wide off the east side of his lot in the southwest quarter of Block 21 for $100. On May 20, 1885, J. W. and I. K. O'Neal sold a strip of land 100 feet wide off the west half of the northwest quarter of Block 21 for $150. And on September 29, 1885, William and Martha McIlroy sold a strip of land 38 feet wide off the west side of their lot in the southwest quarter of Block 21, price not given. The deeds were recorded August 30, 1886.

Railroad construction crews cut into this steeply sloping hillside to level the track bed area, creating a stair-step profile to the property. The land in this location slopes downhill toward the creek, part of a much larger landform that drains from as far east as the town square. The spur track cut down about ten to fifteen feet, displacing significant tonnage of rock and dirt which helped form the rail bed and adjacent level ground later occupied by buildings. The steep slope uphill from the cut yielded at least one water well, which was rocked near the Center Street end and may have provided drinking water for nearby households.

Working with picks, shovels, and mule teams, workers no doubt found this rocky ground a challenge. Few records exist describing the natural topography here. William Campbell's 1928 *100 Years of Fayetteville* document the first store built in Fayetteville (circa 1830). Its planks were riven entirely from one enormous black oak that was felled "just below the big spring south of Frisco depot," (p 11), a site located about one block north of the Quonset property. This large spring is the primary source of water for Town Creek which runs south from Lafayette Street; today the creek emerges from concrete underground conduits only after crossing Center Street near Gregg. But in early Fayetteville, this area was considered impassable. Railroad maps called it an "open ditch." Center Street jogs slightly north as it crosses Gregg going west, a result of early efforts to negotiate this difficult stream crossing. Originally the land west of Gregg probably combined a central stream bed and marshy areas, as well as small bluffs like the stretch along Gregg and the Frisco Multiuse Trail just south of the Center Street jog.

The fifty feet of right of way east of the tracks was not used, since the land fell down the steep hillside. The west fifty feet of right of way was to become the site of many improvements, including the Quonset.

The first record of a structure on this property is found in Campbell's *History* (p 41), which states that in 1895 an ice plant was installed "on the west side of switch track between Center and Meadow." This was the first ice-making machinery in Fayetteville and resulted from a partnership between B. W. Redfern, George Bryan, and W. S. Pollard. Their enterprise, Fayetteville Ice Company, enjoyed a profitable existence. Previously, ice had been cut from rivers and ponds during winter and stored in ice cellars. More recently, ice had been brought in by railway shipment. After testing the market with their venture, these men went on to build a new, larger ice plant at 349 N. West in 1900. They expanded to include cold storage facilities but closed in 1907 after an even larger facility—Arkansas Cold Storage and Ice Company—opened in 1905 facing West Avenue in the present-day location of the Walton Arts Center parking lot.

In 1897, Sanborn Fire Insurance Company drew maps of Fayetteville where insured properties were located. Their records of this block show no buildings at the Center Street end except a residence which remains facing Center Street about eighty feet east of the Quonset. Halfway between Center and Meadow was a wagon warehouse serving Sweitzer Wagon Company. A larger structure at the northwest corner of the property was part of a complex where Sweitzer manufactured wagons, this building

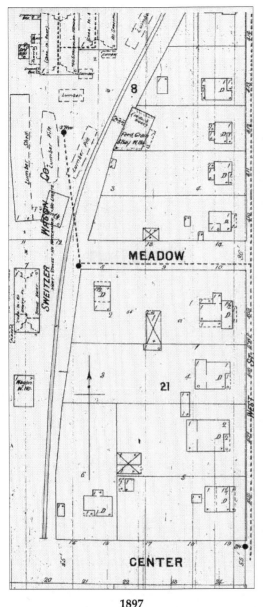

1897

constructed of corrugated iron with earth floor and stove heat. Additional wagon sheds and lumber piles are found farther north along this right of way.

(Sweitzer Wagon Company, according to Campbell's *History* p 38, was the city's first organized business in wagon production. It was headed by E. B. Harrison and Ellis Duncan, starting in 1887 most likely at this location.). Finally, a small residence faced Meadow at the east half of the right of way.

The 1904 Sanborn map shows a similar configuration of warehouses along the west side of the right of way, now under the name of Fayetteville Wagon Wood Company. (Campbell, p 39, states "In 1890, Paddy-Corley Iron Co., of St. Louis, became interested in possibilities here and sent George W. Cleveland here to establish a wagon wood factory, which became known as

Fayetteville Wagon Wood and Lumber Co. Its plant was all over the ground lying south of Arkansas Cold Storage and Ice Co. plant to the Snow Bird Coal Co. It carried an immense stock, had shaping and bending works, dry kilns, and storage sheds and employed a lot of men. It suspended operations here about 1915.") An additional structure had been added mid-block, marked "Hay." Another two structures are shown at the Center Street end, a small building near Gregg Street marked "Office"

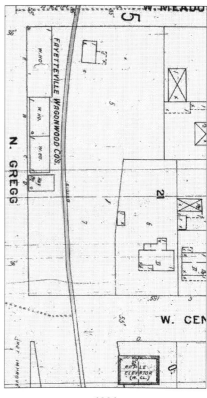

1904

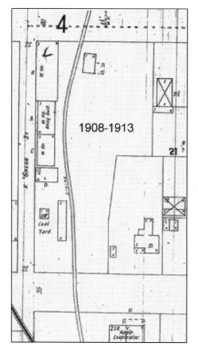

1908-1913

and a long shed near the tracks. The adjacent open area is labeled "Coal Yard."

The Fayetteville City Directory for 1904, the earliest edition available, provides several listings for a business operated by J. H. Williams on Gregg south of Dickson. His name appears under "Coal and Wood," "Flour and Feed," and "Grain and Hay." This operation probably was the hay and coal businesses marked on the Sanborn map for this section of Gregg.

In 1908 and 1913, Sanborn maps do not show the coal yard or office, but Fayetteville Wagon Wood Company continued to occupy the warehouses along the right of way north to Meadow.

Then in 1919, all the warehouses are gone except for one at the northernmost corner. It is marked "miscellaneous merchandise." The small residential structure on Meadow at the east right of way is no longer there.

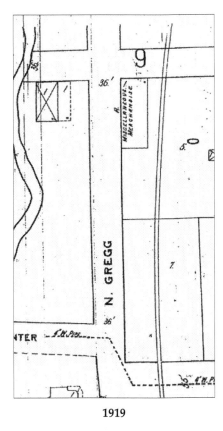

1919

The next available city directory was published for 1927-28. Snowbird Coal Company is shown with an address of Meadow at Gregg. Milton B. "Buck" Slade owned this company and lived with his wife Marie Ilma at 432 N. Washington. The Snowbird Coal Company is also listed in the 1929-30, 1932-33, and 1935-36 directories.

The 1930 Sanborn map shows a double track along this block, with a new siding coming down from Spring Street and stopping at Center. The west right of way land is divided into two sections, with the south third labeled "Cord Wood" and the north two-thirds labeled "Coal." The extra siding may have allowed freight cars loaded with cord wood and coal to sit on the track until emptied. Gregg Street is marked "unpaved". The southeast corner at the intersection of Gregg and Meadow is occupied by a

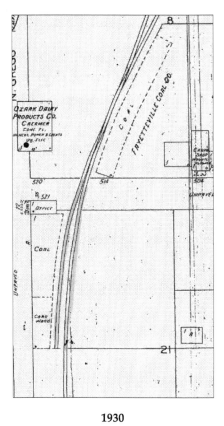

1930

structure labeled "Office." Just north of the office, along a section of Gregg Street no longer in existence, the Ozark Dairy Products Company "Creamer" plant had come into operation. Along the rail bed as it curved northeast from Meadow to Spring Street was another large area marked "Coal" and designated as Fayetteville Coal Company.

Sanborn drawings after 1936 show structures in the location of all current buildings on the property. But these last maps through 1948 were cumulative, meaning these buildings may have appeared after 1936. Quonset structures were not known to have been developed by the U. S. military until World War II, making circa 1941 the earliest plausible Quonset structure at this location.

Both buildings on the 1936–1948 Sanborn map are marked "Feed W'Ho" (warehouse). The second spur shown in 1930 has been removed except for a small portion between the north building and Meadow Street. Fayetteville Coal Company is still so-named, but only north of Meadow. The former "creamer" is now labeled "Buttermilk Ho' (house)."

The 1939 Fayetteville City Directory lists Excelsior Coal Company at the Meadow and Gregg address, owned by John C. McCoy. He lived with his wife just around the corner from the coal yard at 5

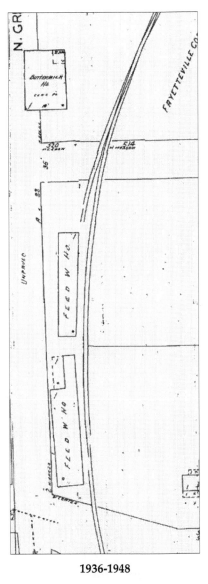

1936-1948

N. West and next door to the Blue Mill Sandwich Shop (9 N. West) operated by Farris and Corrine McCoy. This directory provides no listing for the West Center warehouse.

After 1940, a 16'x96' wood-framed warehouse with sheet metal siding and roof was built at the site of the old coal yard at Meadow and Gregg. While its first use may have been as a feed warehouse, it is believed this warehouse also served the growing food products business located at 509 West Spring.

Food warehousing in this area was established as early as 1920 as Ozark Poultry and Egg Company (Jay Fulbright, M. L. Price). It became part of Jerpe Egg Company by 1932, and in 1951 was under the possession of Swanson's & Sons. Swanson's merged with Campbell Soup in 1959 and Campbell Soup continued production at this location until 1972, when its operations consolidated at their 15th Street facility (now Pinnacle Foods). The old food products plant at 509 West Spring is a grandly renovated structure initially housing Pink Papaya Spa, Lewis & Clark Outfitters, Flying Burrito, Metropolis Hair Salon, and other retail-office operations.

It is not until the city directory's 1951 edition that the Quonset at 530 West Center is listed as the site of Sequoyah Feed and Supply Incorporated, with Harry R. Schultz, President; Donald H. Hunter Vice President; and J. M. Finley, Secretary-Treasurer, as reflected in the last Sanborn map of 1930—1948. Obviously the Quonset existed and served as a feed warehouse without being listed in the city directory until sometime before 1948.

The next available directory, 1955 edition, shows the Quonset as the home of Pillsbury Mills Incorporated. The company's office at 10 ½ S. East was managed by Albert B. McConnell. The Quonset served as the 4-X Feed Store, part of Pillsbury Mills, and was managed by Hubert Parrish with Melvin Parrish as serviceman.

In 1957, E. W. Dozier Roofing Contractor used the Quonset as a warehouse. His ad stated: "Dozier Roofing Contractor – Roofs For Every Purpose, Residential, Industrial, Asphalt Composition, Tar and Gravel, FHA Financing, Bonded and Insured." His office was at 309 St. Charles.

In 1959, Davis Construction Company, with Bryce Davis and Clay B. Yoe as land developers, was using the building. They operated B & C Davis Janitor Supply Company as well.

In 1961, the 530 West Center Street address was joined by a new address, 546 West Center. Davis Construction and its phone number were assigned to the 530 address while B & C Janitor Supply was assigned to 546. These were both part of the Quonset. The 1962 listing no longer includes Davis Construction but B & C Janitor Supply remained at 546 West Center.

Then in 1964, B & C Janitor Supply came under new ownership: Richard D. Foringer, president, Mrs. Evelyn A. Foringer, vice president, and Mrs. Helen Adair, secretary-treasurer. The company remained under this ownership at the Quonset until

1975, when the directory provided the following listing for 17 Gregg Street (basement dock side of the Quonset): Mrs. R. D. Foringer "Disinfectants, Soaps, Mops, Brooms, Brushes, Waxes and Cleaners, Walkway Mats, Swimming Pool Chemicals, Supplies."

From south entry. Space inside Quonset as utilized by Trailside Café, 2009

The 1976 Directory includes no mention of the janitor supply. In its place at 546 W. Center was Pete's Antiques, operated by Loy Peters. This business lasted only two years at this location, at least as far as the city directory shows. Subsequent directories list the property as vacant.

The current owner began renting space in the old wooden warehouse building at Meadow and Gregg in 1982, and at that time the Quonset housed a used clothing store. Immediately preceding this use, there had been a computer repair store in the space for a couple of years. After the current owner gained possession of the entire property from Bryce Davis in 1988, the

Quonset has housed a variety of business endeavors, including a music store, artist studio/gallery (Johnny Schader, Elizabeth Adam), and sign painting shop (Nancy Couch). More recently, this section served as Trailside Café and Tea Room (2009-2011), The Striped Pig vintage resale (2012-2014) and is currently the home of Mayapple Salon & Boutique. The basement hosted a cabinet shop, a cellulose insulation company, and a welding shop, among other things, and currently provides retail space for Guillotine Hair Lounge, Vintage Wolf clothing shop, and The Shed art gallery.

The Quonset is constructed in two levels. The 24' wide upper level facing Center Street is framed by arched steel girders with steel corrugated metal covering. The floor and subfloor are full dimension two-by oak. The south thirty-foot length of the Quonset was finished into a three-room office space with insulation and squared-off lowered ceilings, while the remaining fifty-five feet of the Quonset remained open warehouse space with two large side doors opening toward the railroad siding.

The basement is sixteen feet wide with a little over seven feet clearance to the bottom of the rough-cut oak floor joists. Its underground east wall is formed concrete from eighteen to thirty inches thick. Rough oak beams about 12"x12" sit on same-sized oak posts to provide support to the upper floor. The west wall is supported by concrete piers and oak posts. A non-structural foundation west wall nearly three feet thick along this side is a combination of poured concrete, rubble, and concrete block.

A concrete loading dock runs along the south half of the basement wall, and originally this section of the basement was open to the outside through large sliding doors. A wood-frame structure was built onto the north end of the Quonset, approximately 25'x30'. An attached roof extended from its west side toward Gregg Street, but the slow collapse of a retaining wall along Gregg Street compromised the use of this roofed area and it was removed in 1988 by the current owner. This building includes a small office area and a passage door through the north Quonset wall.

The old wooden warehouse at 541 West Meadow includes large sliding doors along the railroad frontage would have allowed for movement of pallets stacked with feed, Swansons & Sons, and/or Campbell Soup products. One such door remains, while a second opening has been enclosed. At the north end, a door entry with a small porch facing Meadow Street was added in 1982 when this building became the headquarters of Pitts Piano Service Inc. Piano repair and restoration continued in the building until 1993, when the south half was converted into two rental units for music rehearsal studios. Pitts Piano Service vacated the north half in 2006, and the building has since accommodated a repair shop, a second-hand store, and an art studio/gallery. Currently the north half hosts Backspace, a venue created to support community arts programming through events such as music and art shows, readings, performances, and more.

Now partitioned into three rental units, the basement includes original concrete floors and the massive concrete basement wall (east). The old oak posts and beams are now painted white.

By the mid-1990s, the Quonset's upper and lower levels had been subdivided into seven rental units occupied by music groups for rehearsal space. This usage began with Paul Boatright's effort to start a recording studio in 1989, which led to the formation of the group "Punkinhead." Bands occupying rehearsal space in what came to be known as the "Center Street Studios" included Ultra Suede, The Odds, Kind, Grandpa's Goodtime Fandango, Delta Spacemen, Statik, Rofkar, Madhatter, Vox Humana, Lucious Spiller, Dirt Spirits, The Tickle, Plow Musik, Leah & the Mojo Doctors, Rise to Ruin, Vore, and Omega Red (later Hymns). In all, over 80 groups of musical hopefuls rented space in these buildings between 1989 and 2006, when the studio use ended and existing renters were moved to improved rehearsal facilities at Huntsville Road Studios in southeast Fayetteville.

541 West Meadow

Throughout the property's long history, the east side of the right of way remained undeveloped except for the early residence facing Meadow. The hillside grew up in trees and native vegetation. Birds and other wildlife frequented the small woodland area, enjoyed by tenants of the property and by pedestrians and bicyclists who used the old rail bed as a walkway/alleyway.

In 2006, after a long negotiation with the city, a 20'-wide strip along the east property line was donated as a permanent easement to the City of Fayetteville. This allowed for the north-south passage of the Frisco Trail through this block. The owner denied the city its preferred route along the old rail bed because it bisected the 100' wide property along its center.

Facing north along the old rail bed

While some trees were lost due to trail construction, the hillside continues to exude a certain magical charm. Rocks which had framed the old hand-dug well were recovered when dirt was moved for construction and now line an embankment near the trail.

Looking north along the Frisco Trail, at east property line of Quonset property

2006 improvements to the Quonset made it more suitable for a variety of commercial uses. Although cause for lament among carpenters and other building tradesmen who find nothing in these buildings square or plumb, the structures remain sturdy in spite of their age. With the increasing pace of development in the Downtown/Dickson Street area, the Quonset and other buildings will likely be removed at some future date when the property is sold and investors prepare the land for "higher" use. Bulldozers removing these structures will find the old railroad bed well packed into the rocky hillside and a black layer of coal just beneath the ground surface.

The History of Fayette Junction

Hub of Washington County's 1885 – 1935 Timber Boom

Introduction

Although I have been in and out of Fayetteville all my life and many times have traveled through the area now subject of this narrative, I had never heard of Fayette Junction. Neither had any of the people I asked. The site and its history came to my attention in early 2003 as I sought a location to build a workspace complex for service businesses.

But in its day, Fayette Junction served as the center of a bustling enterprise best summed up by its biggest business, Sligo Wagon Wheel Company. From the outside in 2003, the old Sligo building was almost invisible. Not only had it disappeared behind the eager growth of native vegetation, but the building itself seemed to merge into the land as an organic element. But once a visitor braved the forbidding surroundings to venture inside, an astonishing vista awaited.

There, rising up to about 24 feet at the ridge, the vast old warehouse seemed to stretch out forever, its ten-foot side walls lost in distant shadow. The roof framing remained the same strong oak it was at its inception but several of the posts had failed and allowed the roof to sag in three noticeable spots. The concrete slab floor rose and fell in uneven, broken sections. The remains of its last occupant dotted the expanse, pallet stacks of dusty window framing and unfinished louvered doors.

The Sligo building and the surrounding forty acres of Fayette Junction are all that remain of another era, a time when the United States and its eager pioneers could freely exploit natural resources that seemed limitless in its bounty. A significant portion of Fayetteville's wealth grew from the timber boom of 1885-1935.

And then it was gone. It seems the least we can do is to remember it.

North end of Sligo Building at the end of its life, 2003

Fayette Junction

Fayette Junction lies at the heart of present-day south Fayetteville, a 40-acre piece of mostly flat land bordered on the east by South Garland Avenue and along the south by Cato Springs Road (State Highway 265). The north perimeter of Fayette Junction is roughly delineated by Town Creek, and its west side by the main track of the railroad that travels south from Fayetteville to Ft. Smith. On either side of the spur track that once ventured east to St. Paul and Pettigrew from the main line, new apartments and warehouses have sprung up. Cement trucks come and go from the southwest portion of Fayette Junction, hauling loads of "ready-mix" to construction sites in the region. Tangled within these identified uses, a few remaining parcels of land lie forgotten in tall weeds and crumbling structures, all that remains of the site's glory days when the wealth of Fayetteville depended on steel tracks and a

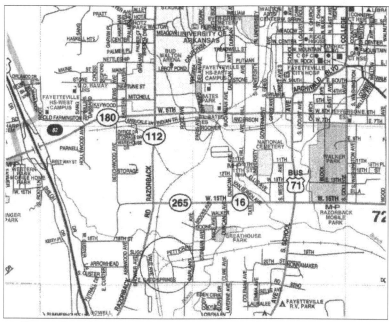

Fayette Junction appears in the circled area, bottom center of map

thriving timber trade.

When these lands of the soon-to-be State of Arkansas began to be surveyed and parceled out in 1834, the 640-acre portion later to contain the forty acres of Fayette Junction was designated "school land." Freedom from private ownership and troublesome homesteads may have contributed to John Butterfield's decision to cross this section with his late 1850s overland mail route on its way from St. Louis south through Fayetteville and on west to San Francisco. In reviewing the earliest maps of this area, one sees the known Butterfield route angling down what is now Brooks Avenue and continuing south along Cato Springs Road toward Hogeye.

A study of the physical contour of land across Fayette Junction leads to the opinion that a stagecoach would have crossed Town Creek near the present-day Brooks Avenue crossing and then climbed to the ridge immediately ahead before angling southwest along the original path of Cato Springs Road. Early history credits Native Americans for this trail, but the actual pathways were obliterated by the construction of the railroad. The subsequent roadway of South Garland and Cato Springs Road skirted the railroad junction with square corners and straight lines that would not have been meaningful to Natives or the Butterfield mail route. We can with fair certainty assert that the Butterfield Stage Line angled directly across the acreage which is the subject of this history.

The first record of private ownership appears in the tax records of 1861, with this forty-acre piece in the hands of Zebulon M. Pettigrew. It appears to have been passed on to his son George A. (or H.) Pettigrew by 1869, when it was valued at $150. In 1883, it sold to J. A. Ferguson who co-founded Washington County Bank in 1884 and established Hill City Lumber Company in 1900. In

1887, valued at $400, the forty acres became the property of the St. Louis and San Francisco Railway, possibly a gift along with many other acres of land that were offered by local businessmen to secure the railway's profitable route. By 1900 the property was valued at $2000, but after 1908 the value was not assessed in the tax record due to railroad exemptions. For fifty years, heavy rail traffic and boom-town hardwood milling operations would cover this piece of land with buildings, sheds, roads, and mountainous stacks of hardwood lumber as ambitious men cut through the virgin forests of Washington, Madison, and Franklin counties.

The Railroad Comes to Fayetteville

As early as 1855, Fayetteville city leaders had recognized the potential profit and growth that railway connections would bring to the rest of the county. The rugged Ozark terrain isolated their fledgling village, making commerce difficult and expensive for necessities and luxuries alike. Goods came north by ox cart from the Arkansas River at Van Buren or Ft. Gibson, Indian Territory, or south from the railhead in Missouri. After the Civil War, in 1868 Arkansas legislators passed a bill granting aid to railroads which in turn prompted the St. Louis and San Francisco to start laying track south from Springfield, Missouri. The Frisco line made it to Fayetteville in 1881with passenger service delayed until the completion of the Winslow tunnel. On July 4, 1882, a brass band and a crowd of 10,000 greeted the first passenger train at the Fayetteville Dickson Street station.

All kinds of goods traveled along the new line from Monett, Missouri to Fort Smith—product of a fourteen-year construction effort—encouraging the hopes of men and families seeking livelihood. The most plentiful and profitable local raw material available for the taking were the old-growth trees. Land sold for $1 per acre with an estimated available merchantable timber of

5000 board feet per acre. A flourishing trade blossomed along the track as the forest fell to the hands of hardworking men. Within the first decade after 1882, West Fork, Woolsey, Brentwood, Winslow, and several long-since vanished whistle stops south of Fayetteville became boom towns where railroad ties, fence posts, and rough-cut lumber were loaded onto railcars.

One of the most ambitious men to exploit the timber trade was Hugh F. McDanield,[1] a railroad builder and tie contractor who had come to Fayetteville along with the Frisco. He bought thousands of acres of land within hauling distance of the railroad and sent out teams of men to cut the timber. By the mid-1880s, after a frenzy of cutting in south Washington County, he turned his gaze to the untapped fortune of timber on the steep hillsides of southeast Washington County and southern Madison County, territory most readily accessed along a wide valley long since leveled by the east fork of White River. Mr. McDanield gathered a group of backers[2] and the state granted a charter September 4, 1886, giving authority to issue capital stock valued at $1.5 million, which was the estimated cost to build a rail line through St. Paul

---

[1] Hugh McDanield, b 1843 to B. F. and Sarah (Terrell), fought for the Union in the Civil War, worked in mercantile trade in Kansas City until 1873, built the Kansas Midland Railway from Kansas City to Topeka, and then operated a ranch in west Texas. After completing the Texas Western Railway in 1877, he turned his attention to Northwest Arkansas and began selling ties in 1881. He bought, logged, and sold thousands of acres of Washington County land and later Madison and Franklin counties over the next seven years and made a fortune furnishing the Santa Fe Railway nearly all its ties. He is credited as founder of St. Paul by the 1889 Goodspeed. He died in Fayetteville in 1888 of a month-long, unnamed illness at age 45.

[2] including F. H. Fairbanks, J. F. Mayes, and J. S. Van Hoose, along with his brother J. S. McDanield, all of Fayetteville, and D. B. Elliott of Delaney, J. Pickens of Eversonville, Missouri, J. W. Brown of Brentwood, and another brother, B. F. McDanield of Bonner Springs Kansas.

and on to Lewisburg, which was a riverboat town on the Arkansas River near Morrilton. McDanield began surveys while local businessman J. F. Mayes worked with property owners to secure rights of way. "On December 4, 1886, a switch was installed in the Frisco main line about a mile south of Fayetteville, and the spot was named Fayette Junction." Within six months, 25 miles of track had been laid east by southeast through Baldwin, Harris, Elkins, Durham, Thompson, Crosses, Delaney, Patrick, Combs, and finally St. Paul.

This 1908 map shows the "wye" and Vale Post Office. Washington County Plat, County Archives

Soon after, in 1887, the Frisco bought the so-called "Fayetteville and Little Rock" line from McDanield. It was estimated that in the first year McDanield and partners shipped out more than $2,000,000 worth of hand-hacked white oak railroad ties at an approximate value of twenty-five cents each. Mills ran day and night as people arrived "by train, wagon, on horseback, even afoot" to get a piece of the action along the new track, commonly referred to as the "St. Paul line." Saloons, hotels, banks, stores, and services from smithing to tailoring sprang up in rail stop communities.

As the Fayetteville & Little Rock track extended to Dutton and its final easternmost point at Pettigrew in 1897, local sawmills processed massive logs of oak, walnut, maple, and hickory into rough lumber before it was loaded onto the railcars. "Wagons loaded with hardwood timber—cross ties, fence posts, rives, felloes, sawed lumber to be finished into buggy and wagon wheels and spokes, single trees, neck yokes, handles for hammers and plows, and building materials" streamed into the rail yards along the St. Paul line.

All the timber from points east and south poured through Fayette Junction. The "wye" of tracks there formed fertile ground for milling, warehousing, and other specialized operations of the timber trade. Men worked at a frantic pace to capitalize on the conquest of such a valuable resource. Buildings sprang up at the Junction, primarily hardwood milling operations. Today a visitor to the site can find the remains of some of these early structures. Facing Garland Avenue just north of the vacated spur track to St. Paul remains the vast concrete floor of the old warehouse of the Sligo Wagon Wood Company, built circa 1900. Another original building remains at the northwest corner of Fayette Junction with the faint words "Brower Veneer" fading on its sheet metal walls.

Overnight, men became wealthy according to their ability to take advantage of the timber trade. With the railroad came enormous growth and the need for more homes, churches, offices, and commercial enterprise. Sufficient supply of building materials depended upon ever more distant timber harvest and upon the increasingly mechanized production of lumber. Peter Van Winkle had established the first lumber mills in the region by the 1850s, powered by oxen with operations in the Clifty area of eastern Benton County. By 1858, his new steam boiler venture included a shingle machine, door and window factory, and a cabinet shop. Most of the lumber for pre-Civil War Fayetteville buildings came from the Van Winkle mill.

After the war, a fledgling lumber industry began to grow in Fayetteville, and in the 1870s, Alexander Hendry and D. B. Bradley built a planing mill "down under the hill east of the square, corner of Rock and Mill." (This location suggests use of Town Branch to drive water wheels, since the town's flour and feed mill also occupied this area.) In the 1880s, Hendry and Bradley's apprentice Albert M. Byrnes bought out Dale Lumber Company and got into his own planing business, and by 1905 had joined with other men to form Northwest Arkansas Lumber Company (later sold to Kelley Brothers Lumber Company). Other concerns sprang up: Hill City Lumber Company (1900), Fayetteville Lumber and Cement (1903), and Wages Brothers Construction Company (1918).

In turn-of-the-century Fayetteville, specialized products of hardwood such as handles and wooden wagon parts were milled and shipped nationwide by several entrepreneurs including Pitkin & Mayes Lumber Company, Charlesworth Hardwood Lumber Company; W. N. Jones; Sandford Hardwood Lumber Company; Fayetteville Wagon Wood and Lumber Co.; J. H. Phipps Lumber Company; Byrnes Lumber Company, and Ferguson Lumber Company. (This is the same Ferguson who sold the original 40-acre tract that became Fayette Junction. Ferguson's interests included the Red Star Spoke Factory, makers of wagon and automobile wheel spokes, which began in 1902 at Red Star at its remote location east of Pettigrew in Madison County but moved to

Fayetteville in 1909.)

This frenzy of lumber and milling enterprises fed off the virgin forests of southern Washington and Madison counties, with mills and factories located at various sites around Fayetteville. White oak was preferred for railroad ties while red oak was the resilient wood of choice for wagon stock, especially bows, hubs, and spokes. Other woods milled included walnut, hickory, ash, and cherry. All of the trains carrying lumber from the St. Paul line steamed through Fayette Junction, where loads of posts, ties, and raw materials for milling jammed the side tracks. The 1904 Fayetteville City Directory authors summarize: "Those industries which have to do with the manufacture of various articles from hard wood timber are probably among Fayetteville's most important enterprises. There are four factories devoted to the manufacture of wood wagon materials alone. Their product is shipped to many foreign parts, to the new Island possessions, as well as to every large manufacturing center in our own country."

The Men and Mills at Fayette Junction

Pitkin & Mayes, the first milling business at Fayette Junction, advertised as manufacturers of hardwood lumber in the 1892 *Arkansas State Gazetteer & Business Directory*. Erastus Pitkin and John F. Mayes were the proprietors, the same J. F. Mayes who originally invested and secured rights-of-way for the St. Paul line. Pitkin & Mayes sold its Fayette Junction operations to Sligo Wagon Wood Company sometime around 1905. No doubt there were other hard wood business concerns at Fayette Junction before 1895 since the line to St. Paul opened in 1887, but no documents have been found to describe them.

The following hardwood operations in railroad ties and wagon wood parts were listed in the 1904 Fayetteville City Directory as having "works" at Fayette Junction (with no hint of the date of their origin): Charlesworth Hardwood Lumber Company; W. N. Jones; Sandford Hardwood Lumber Company; Pitkin & Mayes, and Sligo Wagon Wood Company. By 1907, they were joined at the junction by J. P. Brower Veneer Company. Subsequent sections of this article describe each company in turn.

Charlesworth Hardwood Lumber Company

William Charlesworth built a handle factory in 1902, with milling works located at Fayette Junction. Born in Ohio to parents both born in England, Charles[3] married Calona Yoes in 1884, her family early settlers in northwest Arkansas. He was among the first businessmen to jump into trade made possible by the new railway. Within the first year of St. Paul's existence, Charlesworth & Harrigan operated a feed store there. In the 1900 Madison County census, the couple lived in Kentucky Township (centered around Pettigrew), had three living children (four had died) and a 19-year-old female hired hand named America McAdoo. In 1904, the family lived at 533 N. Willow in Fayetteville. The Charlesworth Hardwood Lumber company had offices at #3, 6 West Center. The family was also listed in Fayetteville for the 1910 census, although in 1912 William was serving as president of the St. Paul bank. The couple had two more daughters; one of them, Myrl Vesta Charlesworth, graduated Fayetteville High School in 1919. William sold his milling company in 1918 to J. L Stice who subsequently built up the business specializing in hickory handles for the ax, pick, hoe, and spade. By 1913, the Stice mill relocated away from Fayette Junction to about one mile northwest of the

---

[3] William was born in 1859, died 1941; Calona born Feb 16, 1867, died Jul 13, 1958. Their children were Claude later of Ojai CA, b. 1887, d. 1976, married Bernice Brogoan d. 1944; Darwin C. later of Springdale then Tulsa, b. 1893 d 1983, married Naomi Miller; Jim (James) R. b. 1898, d 1967 Springdale; Myrl b. ca 1901 Fayetteville; Yvonne, Tulsa.

square, alongside the tracks on Frisco Street at the current Gregg Street crossing of North Street. Stice was out of operation by 1936.

W. N. Jones

William Newton ("Newt" or "W.N.") Jones was born April 7, 1851, in Washington County, one of eight surviving children of Claiborne and Jennie Tallent Jones, recently arrived from Hawkins County, Tennessee. Claiborne was a Baptist minister and farmer who settled in the Durham area. William married Matilda E. Lewis (b 1855), daughter of early Fayetteville settlers G. W. and Elizabeth Lewis.[4]

Newton Jones became entangled in a feud of sorts. Subjected to life-threatening shootings by Calvin "Bud" Gilliland, Jones took matters into his own hands in 1874 when he rode up into a public gathering in the Middle Fork valley and, without dismounting, leveled his rifle and shot Gilliland dead. He escaped into Texas for nearly two years before returning to face his crime. On his return, a posse led by Gilliland's brother attempted to kill him by laying wait along the roadway, but only succeeded in killing his nephew. Jones stood trial and was found not guilty, most likely due to the knowledge that Bud Gilliland had threatened his life.

With all that behind him and pursuing a livelihood in farming, Newton Jones opened the first business at Delaney as soon as the railroad arrived. "In February 1887, Wm. N. Jones opened the first store in a tent." Two years later, he had joined with Capt. A. L. Thompson in Jones & Thompson, a firm "doing a thriving business and also has a branch store at Combs' station, and sells the principal part of the goods on the railroad." Jones was credited with the establishment of the town of Delaney. By 1904, Jones and

---

[4] Children of William and Matilda were Eddit T., Nora D., Minnie, Maudie, and Lonnie. See Goodspeed p 1100.

family lived at 5 South School where he was also the proprietor of Ozark Livery Stables at the same location (southwest corner of School and Center). The stables, which hosted weekly livestock auctions, first occupied a half block of land between Mountain and Center along Church Street, then moved west two blocks. W. M. Simmons assisted in the stable operation which included offices for veterinarian surgeon Dr. Frederick Burkey. The Jones family reportedly later moved west to locations in Wyoming, Utah, and Washington state. There is no available information about the extent of his hardwood business at Fayette Junction.

Sandford Hardwood Lumber Company

Claude Herbert Sandford (b. Dec 21, 1876, d. Aug 4, 1933) came to Fayetteville as early as April 1897 from Parkerville, Kansas with his father Samuel Sandford, an immigrant from England. In the 1900 census, Claude was listed as a boarder at 129 S. West; his wife Lillian of Manhattan, Kansas (b. 1877, d. Jun 16, 1948) joined him in 1903.[5] Samuel Sandford and Ellis Duncan bought property together in April 1897, located near the Frisco line around Dickson Street. After Samuel's initial partnership with E. Pitkin and Ellis Duncan in the Ozark Wagon Company and a hard wood operation at Fayette Junction, Samuel and Claude Sandford built a foundry and iron works in 1905, located at 603 W. Dickson, which continued in operation through the 1920s, a location now approximately occupied by the parking lot of George's Majestic Lounge. Sandford's operations at Fayette Junction were undocumented.

---

[5] A brother A. G. Sandford also came to Fayetteville, but moved to Okmulgee OK in the early 1940s. Claude's three children were Claude H. Sandford Jr. (California), Mary (Bob) Saladino (Fayetteville), and Ralph (Mike) Sandford (Fayetteville) (as of 1948).

Pitkin & Mayes

J. Frank Mayes

J. Frank Mayes (born in Fayetteville March 16, 1862) obtained a Bachelor of Arts degree at the University in 1883. His father, William Zarro Mayes, was the contractor responsible for the construction of Old Main. W. Z., who died at age 53 in 1888, came to Fayetteville from Tennessee at age eight with parents "Uncle" Johnny (Rev. John) and Sarah McGhee Mayes. In 1854, Rev. Mayes founded First Baptist Church of Fayetteville, now located at the corner of Dickson and College.[6] Beginning in 1897, J. Frank served as chief of the Fayetteville fire department and was responsible for the purchase of the city's first fire wagon (horse drawn). He served about 30 years as a member of the state executive committee for the Republican Party. He was U. S. Marshall of the Western District of Arkansas for eight years. At one time, he was a candidate for governor and for Congress from the Third Congressional District on the Republican ticket. He was a member of the Masonic lodge and Knights of Pythias, and an active member of the Baptist church.

Among his other adventures, Frank Mayes joined a group of men for the run on the opening of the Cherokee Strip in 1893. None of the party are believed to have actually filed a claim. In 1909 he drove a Flanders roadster, and in 1919 he owned a Willys Knight. Later historian W. J. Lemke, investigating a grist mill site along

---

[6] Two sisters of J. Frank were Mrs. James Carlile of Fayetteville and Mrs. Nora Simmons of Hot Springs (1938). He died March 22, 1938, in Manitou, Colorado, after moving there for his health. He had three children by his first wife Sarah Mulholland: Allan Mayes of Hollywood; Ruth Mayes Lane of Columbia, SC, and Mildred Mayes Munro of Colorado Springs. His second wife was Mary (b. July 22, 1854, d. Oct 22, 1927).

Wilson Lake Road believed to be Fayetteville's first, discovered a fine old buggy in a shed on the property, and was told that it had belonged to Frank Mayes "when he was fire chief of Fayetteville."

Erastus L. Pitkin

Erastus Pitkin of Pitkin & Mayes and of Ozark Wagon Company was the ninth generation of Pitkins originating with Wyllyam Pitkyn (born 1557) of Berkhamsted, Hertfordshire, England. This lineage settled in the Hartford, Connecticut area around 1661. Erastus was born in Vermont in 1824, and married Emily Barnes (b. 1830 Ohio, d. January 5, 1910). Erastus moved to Birmingham, Iowa by the early 1850s, serving as a founding member of the city council in 1856. Certain skills and persons he knew there were to be part of his later life in Arkansas.

Bricks fired in a kiln on the Glotfelty farm were used to build an 80' chimney for a Birmingham sawmill which E. L. Pitkin and C. L. Moss purchased in 1853. Soon after, they added a grist and flour mill to the operation. In January 1860, Erastus' second child and only son Joel M. was born, but sometime later that year, Erastus sold out his share of the mill to Mr. Moss. In the 1860 census he declared himself a "merchant" with $1200 in real estate and $400 in personal assets. His household included his wife, a daughter age ten, and a 23-year-old female servant. The 1870 Iowa census shows he remained at Birmingham throughout the Civil War, producing two more daughters during the decade and substantially improving his financial situation. He is described in the census as a "dry goods merchant" with $19,600 in real estate and $12,550 in personal assets.

The first evidence of Mr. Pitkin's arrival in Arkansas came with the opening of the railroad in the early 1880s, when he bought up most of the land for a square mile (Section 16 of T14N, R30W) along the banks of Mill Creek where it enters the White River (west fork) and south along the river valley in an area known as "Woolsey" (just south of West Fork, Washington County). In June 1882 William T. Woolsey sold 90 acres of land to Pitkin, who bought another 90 acres from Mary Jane Karnes. There, near a large spring that enters the river from an eastern bluff face, Erastus established a sawmill and grist mill immediately west of the railroad tracks.[7] Later records show this mill in operation by his son Joel, who in turn leased it for five years to James Karnes in 1886. On May 21, 1884, the Pitkin post office was established, as well as Pitkin School, Washington County No. 3. The U. S. Department of the Interior Geological Survey Map of 1898 lists both Woolsey and Pitkin, with Woolsey slightly southwest of Pitkin, although various other records refer to Pitkin and Woolsey as the same location.

Erastus bought and sold many parcels of land in southern Washington County, presumably to profit from the timber. In some purchases, he partnered with his son, while at least in one parcel, he partnered with Nelson Glotfelty[8]; most of these timber lands were along Bethlehem Road (WC 237). Erastus probably lived for a time in the middle of a 160-acre piece on Sugar Mountain Road (WC 156), which he and his wife Emily purchased on June 21, 1886. (They sold the property to J. Wallace Ferguson on February 18, 1903.) In 1888, he patented 200 acres in Madison County through the Arkansas School Lands sales.

---

[7] As of 2021, this building remained standing and in use as Ozark Custom Butchering.

[8] Nelson Glotfelty and his wife Armanda signed their affidavit at Van Buren County, Iowa, for the sale of this land in 1903. The property was bought as public land in 1888, Nelson listed with Erastus on the certificate of register at the Harrison land office. Nelson was born Jan 7, 1842, in Somerset PA and died Oct 30, 1893, in Birmingham IA. His family never moved to Arkansas.

As soon as the railroad opened, Erastus Pitkin and his old friend from Iowa, Nelson Glotfelty, launched a hardwood lumber operation in West Fork, which they named Pitkin & Glotfelty. They immediately wrote to the Springfield Wagon Company, Springfield Missouri, asking for prices on their "log wagons," a specialized heavy-duty, independent-axle wagon used to haul logs (1883). Whether they intended to market these wagons to the men engaged in the massive timber harvest going on around them or to use the Springfield product as a pattern by which to manufacture their own is not known. Perhaps they simply wanted to purchase wagons for logging their own land.

By 1895, Pitkin & Mayes Company (E. Pitkin and J. Frank Mayes) had established offices at Room 17, Bank of Fayetteville building, with hardwood milling operations located at Fayette Junction. The mill buildings were located at the north end of the "wye" where the St. Paul track split from the southbound Frisco line. The site, later to be Brower Veneer, included a woodworking building with saw mill and steam vat, six warehouses, an open area for "piles of hardwood lumber," a boiler room, a water tower, a bending facility with its own steam vat, and a large pond. A small office building and warehouse were located near the tracks across from the Frisco water tower. They manufactured and warehoused wooden wagon parts.

In 1896, Erastus Pitkin joined with Ellis Duncan to establish the Ozark Wagon Company and served as its president, although by 1904 Ellis Duncan was its manager. That same year Mr. Pitkin was listed as partner in the brick manufacturing business of Algire & Pitkin, located at South and East Streets.[9]

---

[9] Goodspeed p. 256 notes a "Willard Algine (sic) & Co." brick and stone mason business (1889). Willard, born 1845, fought with the Illinois

Erastus Pitkin's last home in 1904 was at or near the current address of 1335 South School, a property sold to him by Willard Algire. The existing yellow brick structure at this location may have been his house. Ozark Wagon Company went bankrupt in 1909, which may or may not have been somehow connected with E. Pitkin's decline.

That same year Willard Algire returned to Iowa with his second wife, Emma Caldonia Fallin. Record of Erastus Pitkin's wife's death appeared in local newspapers in January 1910, stating that she was buried at Combs Chapel Cemetery, Fayetteville. Washington County probate records include a letter of administration signed February 23, 1911, assigned J. T. Taylor as administrator of Pitkin's estate. His heirs were Joel, Mrs. J. C.

---

infantry in the Civil War, but his father was from Arkansas. His first wife Lillie Topping was born in Maryland, but her father was from Ireland. In 1884, they came to Fayetteville from Birmingham, Iowa. Willard bought 70 acres just south of Fayetteville and began his brick business. Sometime in the late 1880s, Mr. Algire built Yoes' two-story brick store in West Fork (*Flashback* Aug 1961, p 26).

Thom (?), and "the heirs of Mrs. Broyles." He would have been 87. [10] A grave marker at the Maple Hill Cemetery Birmingham, Van Buren County, Iowa names both Erastus and his wife Emily Barnes with her death January 2, 1910, and his death April 1, 1910.

Evidence suggests that the end of Pitkin & Mayes at Fayette Junction resulted from fire at the mill. While their operations are described in Sanborn maps published in 1904, subsequent maps from 1913 describe the mill location: "Buildings along here burnt 1904."

It is ironic that property co-owned by the Fayetteville fire chief would have gone up in flames, but saw mills were notorious fire hazards. By 1913, the property had become J. P. Brower's operation. It is possible Pitkin & Mayes were engaged in hardwood milling here as early as 1887 when the St. Paul line opened. Considering their record as experienced businessmen, it seems unlikely that they would have failed to profit from the rush of enterprise going on around them.

Approximately 12,000 wagons were believed in use in the four-county area in 1888, and the mill supplied parts for the largest wagon manufacturer in the region. At the most, Pitkin & Mayes could have been in operation for fifteen years in wagon parts

---

[10] The children of Erastus Sr. and Emily B. were Rose L. (1850), Alta (1857), Joel M. (1860), Mary (1861), and Maggie (1865). Joel married Lillie Dell (1871– Jul 5, 1938) of Woolsey/Pitkin, where they produced two sons, Lee and Hugh, and two daughters Mrs. Stella (Charles) Robinson and Hattie Caudle. Their son Lee Pitkin, (b. 1886, d. Apr 30, 1965) married Anna (Annie) Caudle (b.1886, d. May 7, 1969). Lee worked as a railway agent and died at Centerton (Benton County). Their three children were Mrs. Joe Swift, Alma Pitkin, and Mrs. Jake Woods. Anna's sister Mildred Caudle remained at West Fork.

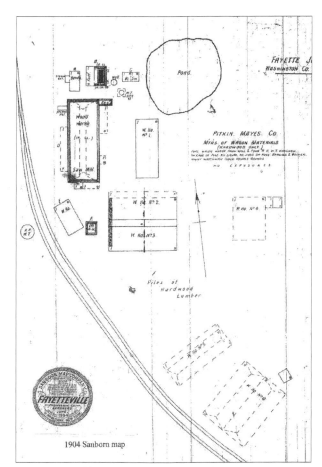

1904 Sanborn map

milling or some aspect of the hardwood lumber trade at Fayetteville Junction.

Sligo Wagon Wood Company

From his 1928 perspective, W. C. Campbell wrote: "In 1895, Frank Mayes and E. Pitkins opened a hardwood mill at the "Y," called the business Pitkins and Mayes, and later sold to Sligo Iron Co. of St. Louis. This company sent Alex McCartney here to open up and see if the business could be made to pay. Mr. McCartney soon proved that, and today Sligo Wagon Wood and Iron Co. factory is one of the show places of Fayetteville's suburbs. Mr. McCartney has had the plant rebuilt four times, each time enlarging. They have had from 30 to 85 men on the yearly payroll, and the business done averages $300,000 annually. Mr. McCartney has been in continuous management thirty-three years." According to a 1905 corporate resolution signed by Sligo's board president T. P. Conant in St. Louis, Mr. Alexander McCartney's establishment and subsequent operations of Sligo Wagon Wood Company were kicked off with a $10,000 allowance of company funds.

It may or may not be accurate that Sligo bought out Pitkin & Mayes. If its mill was destroyed by fire, not much of Pitkin and Mayes would have been left at the northwest Fayette Junction site except perhaps finished inventories in warehouses and assorted equipment in outlying buildings. Sligo's operations were to take place in a different location at Fayette Junction, on the eastern tip of the "wye" where it crossed South Garland and headed to St. Paul. Perhaps Pitkin & Mayes were responsible for the early warehouse at the Sligo site.

Competition was indeed fierce when Mr. McCartney took up the wagon wood business in the name of Sligo. There is no account of how many hardwood lumber enterprises were producing wooden wagon parts in the nation, but petroleum-powered vehicles were gradually gaining favor. Slowly, the wagon industry started to lose ground. For example, Paddy-Corley Iron Company of St. Louis had sent start–up managers as early as 1890 to establish Fayetteville Wagon Wood Company, located at the present day site of the Nadine Baum Learning Center of the Walton Arts Center along West Avenue between Spring and Meadow and spreading south across Meadow onto the hillside above what is now Gregg St. Their facilities covered "all the ground lying south of Arkansas Cold Storage and Ice Co plant to the Snow Bird Coal Co." and "carried an immense stock, had shaping and bending works, dry kilns, and storage sheds, and employed a lot of men." Competition and the progress of automobiles took its toll even on such a respected and expansive operation; Paddy-Corley closed down in 1915.

The Fayette Junction mill site developed by Sligo was included in the 1904 Sanborn Fire Insurance Company map, identified as the property of Sligo Wagon Wood Company. By this map, the mill occupied a large building about 130' x 70' at the Garland Avenue crossing of the St. Paul track. To obtain sufficient water for operation of their steam boiler and for fire protection, the mill property's owners diverted a spring branch flowing northeast across the land, creating a large pond before it reached Town Creek. Additional water for drinking came from a hand-dug well, site unknown. The 1904 map shows a steam boiler and engine in a small structure having iron siding and a 60' iron chimney at the southeast corner of the building.

Perhaps hastened by the Pitkin & Mayes fire losses, the involvement of Sanborn maps and insurance coverage for Sligo and other concerns signaled an end to the cracker-jack period of timber industry enterprise characterized by the sell-it-from-a-tent rush for profits that had held sway since 1882. By 1900, the easy money—hungry markets for railroad ties and fence posts and 40-inch diameter oak standing twenty feet from the rail bed—was gone; a more experienced and calculating management style hedged all bets as operations became wealthier and more complex.

Subsequent Sanborn Fire Insurance maps for the Sligo site in 1908, 1913, 1919, and 1930 show a progression of facilities with outbuildings for machine shop, storage sheds, warehousing of wagon wood parts, and ultimately a "fireproof" building of brick where new boiler furnaces were housed. The first boilers were located in a small brick structure at the southeast corner of the remaining concrete floor, although the 1913 map shows a second boiler building located several yards away from the larger building and alongside the railroad tracks. The 1919 map shows a coal bin between this small "fireproof" building (brick walls, concrete roof and floor) and the tracks; earlier maps describe the furnace fuel as wood shavings. Sanborn map notes comment on the presence of a night watchman but the lack of lights, clock, and

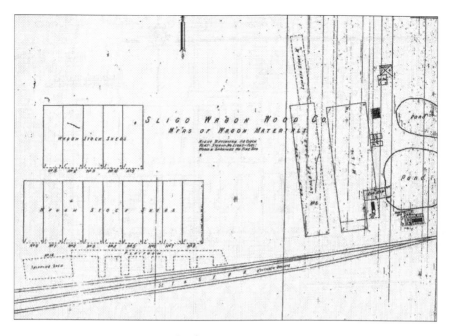

Sanborn 1913

fire apparatus until 1919, when a "Newman Port." clock was added, with "five stations, half hourly rounds" plus city water in a 150' one-inch hose. By the 1930 map, electric lights had been added and additional city water hydrants.

Sligo's Alexander McCartney

Mr. McCartney came to Fayetteville as a native of County Armagh, Ireland, with his wife Mary Ann McKibben Murphy of St. Louis. At least two children were born in St. Louis at late as 1896, so evidently Mr. McCartney worked for some time with Sligo Iron Store Company before coming to Fayetteville. Yet in the corporate papers authorizing him as their agent in Washington County Arkansas, Sligo refers to him as a resident of Fayetteville (1905).

Sligo Iron Store Company of St. Louis served as the wholesale/retail outlet of iron goods in service to the westward settlement migration and continues operations today. In 1984, its heir Sligo Inc. published a brief history of their company on the occasion of its 150th anniversary.

> When St. Louis was first being recognized as the gateway to the West—the staging area for all pioneers headed toward fresh horizons and the new frontier—two enterprising Irish immigrants decided it was the place to seek new opportunity. ...It was 1834 and the thick Irish brogues heard in the large warehouse on North Second Street belonged to Messrs. Lyon and Shorb. The two named the fledgling business 'Sligo & Tyrone Iron Store' after their respective home counties... The great need of a growing country, iron, was their principal merchandise...for wheels, horseshoes, horseshoe nails, and plows. ...The store was filled with neat stacks of iron bars, iron slabs, wheels and plowshares.

The 19th century Sligo Iron Store Company served as an outlet for the iron manufactured in the furnaces of Pennsylvania and no doubt other locations including the Sligo furnaces of nearby Dent County, Missouri. As the pre-eminent supplier of a much-needed commodity, Sligo of St. Louis and Sligo furnaces were widely recognized. For example, an archive of business papers of the Gideon-Anderson Lumber & Mercantile Company, which operated sawmills for the lumber trade in southeast Missouri and northeast Arkansas, include papers from Sligo Iron Store Company of St. Louis. In 1891, when Tipton, Missouri residents placed a document-filled tin box "time capsule" inside an iron column to be part of a new bank building, the contents included communications from Sligo Iron Company. In 1904, "Sligo Furnace" was mentioned among the representatives of the local chemical industry at a gala banquet hosted by the St. Louis Chemical Society on the occasion of the Louisiana Purchase

Exposition. The "Frisco Travelers," a businessmen's association of Rolla and St. James Missouri included "Sligo iron company" in its annual meeting program, described as a "prominent business in St. Louis."

When Alexander McCartney arrived in Washington County with Sligo Iron Store Company money in hand, he did more than seek profitable returns from milling operations in Fayette Junction. Mortgage records of 1895 show that Sligo Iron Store Company bought out John W. Moll and Moll Brothers, for a sum of $1, at a location "25' off the north end of lot #6 Block 13 in Springdale... [and including] all finished and unfinished wagons, all the raw material both iron, wood, and lumber, and all stock of whatsoever and now on hand...and two wagons situated at Blewford in the hands of Charles W. Berry & Company...and also an account due from the Fayetteville Wagon Wood and Lumber Company."

It is not known whether Alexander's original intent in traveling to Washington County had been only to collect the Moll Brother's debt. Perhaps he returned to St. Louis from this assignment with promising reports of the timber boom, thus sending St. Louis Iron Store Company onto a new venture not previously planned. Or perhaps this was simply the iron industry's latest thrust for profits in the tradition of American ambition, since the partnership of iron and hardwood served a vigorous market for everything from wagons and tools to pianos and ice boxes. In any case, by 1906, in a speech to the University student body, professor of economics and sociology Dr. Charles Hillman Brough (elected governor of Arkansas in 1916) named Sligo Wagon Wood Company among "six enterprising firms" to have capitalized on the fertile timber trade. "There is no business in Fayetteville more lucrative in proportion to the capital invested than the hardwood lumber business," he stated. He remarked that with an approximate

This is the north end of the Sligo building shown previously at the end of its life. From company price list brochure

investment of $600,000, these companies "cut last year about 200 million feet of timber, which, on the basis of 8000 feet to the car, represents a shipment of 150 trainloads of lumber from Fayetteville."

Alexander established himself and Sligo firmly in the center of the Fayetteville business community, even though his company's operations were carried out at Fayette Junction which lay outside the city limits. Sligo Wagon Wood Company had offices #1-2 at the McIlroy Building on the Square. Alexander served in 1913 as Commander for Baldwin Commandery Number 4 Knight Templars (Mason) and as a "ruling elder" for the First Presbyterian Church U. S. He and his son Norman were among 23 "Fayetteville Business Men" whose photographs were featured in the September 1919 issue of *Midland Magazine*, listed as manager and assistant manager, respectively, of Sligo Wagon Wood Company. A Sligo ad was featured in the 1920 Fayetteville City Directory, and—ironically—one historian reminisced that in 1920,

Sligo Iron Store Company

ESTABLISHED 1834

Importer, Jobber and Manufacturers' Agent

In the following Lines of Merchandise:

Iron and Steel, Heavy Hardware, Wagon and Vehicle Wood, Trimmings and Mountings For Carriages, Coaches and Automobiles. Paints, Brushes and Varnishes, Scrapers, Barrows and Shovels, Transmission Machinery, Belting, Hose and Packing, Saws and Saw Mill Supplies, Blacksmiths' Coal. Car loads.

Company price list, in possession of author

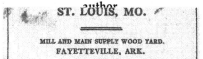

ST. LOUIS, MO.

MILL AND MAIN SUPPLY WOOD YARD.
FAYETTEVILLE, ARK.

Sligo owned one of only fifteen Dodge vehicles in the county.[11]

Norman McCartney joined Mitchell Holt as co-owner of the Dodge dealership, served as treasurer, trustee, and elder for the Presbyterian Church, and co-founded the American Legion *Lynn Shelton Post No. 27* in 1919. Norman married Elizabeth Overstreet, was an infantry first lieutenant in World War I, and for 25 years was president of McCartney-Lewis-Faucette, Inc., a local real estate and insurance firm which still bears his name. He served as a trustee on the board of directors for City Hospital and as advisor to the Kappa Sigma fraternity, also as a board member for Evergreen Cemetery, and was a long-time member of the Fayetteville Rotary. Alexander and his wife Mary Ann had six children; she died in 1940 and he died in 1946. Norman McCartney died in 1965.

A 1922 Sligo Iron Store Company price list shows the Fayette Junction operation, and a 1925 photograph shows the company's workers lined up behind the Fayette Junction mill building.

---

[11] Alexander and Mary McCartney had four daughters and two sons: Ruth (Mrs. J. M.) White, d. Mar 28, 1970 (one daughter Mrs. Frank Proctor of Alexandria VA, with 3 children); Norman; Jess (Mrs. Paul C.) Williams Sr.; Isabelle (Mrs. Howard "Harry") Shultz d. Jan 23, 1954 (Mr. Shultz was executor of Mary's estate and was on faculty at the UA Music Department); Stella (Mrs. Ben H.) Stone; and Paul E. McCartney of Ft. Smith.

(Shiloh Museum) The 1930 Fayetteville City Directory is the last mention of Sligo Wagon Wood Company. On the 1936 Sanborn Fire Insurance maps, the old mill building was occupied by Hargis Canneries for can storage, with the vicinity of the brick structure labeled "office."

Sligo remains an ongoing enterprise. The focus of Sligo Inc. in the 21st century is the marketing of over 30,000 metal products.

Fayetteville Business Men in the following Groups, or mentioned elsewhere in this review are recognized leaders in their respective lines and leaders in all movements to advance the material interests of the city and surrounding country.

—PHOTOS BY J. H. FIELD

Fred F. Borden, Sec. & Mgr. Ozark Grocery Co., and President B. M. C.   W. J. Reynolds, Sec. J. H. Phipps Lumber Co.   C. W. Appleby, Appleby Bros.   W. J. Hamilton, A. C. Hamilton & Company.   Alex McCartney, Mgr. Sligo Wagon Wood Co.   W. G. McCoy, Sec. and Mgr. N. W. Ark. Lumber Co.

J. C. Futrall, Pres. U of A.   Art Lewis, Pres. First Nat. Bank.   T. L. Hart, Cashier Arkansas Nat. Bank.   H. K. Wade, Cashier McIlroy Banking Co.   Bruce Holcomb, Cashier Nat. Bank.   C. T. Harding, First Sec. B. M. C.

F. M. Patrick, V-Pres. Ozark Poultry & Egg Co.   Geo. Appleby, Appleby Bros.   Norman McCartney, Asst. Mgr. Sligo Wagon Wood Co.   A. R. Mintun, Simpson-Mintun Company.   A. C. Hamilton Jr., A. C. Hamilton & Co.   W. H. McIlroy, Mgr. Ark. Cold Storage & Ice Co.

Martin Nelson, Dean of U. of A.   Scott Hamilton, A. C. Hamilton & Company.   W. M. Simpson, Simpson-Mintun Co.   F. N. Gray, Mgr. & Treas. Fayetteville Mer. Co.   W. P. McNair, Frisco Agent.

Brower Veneer Mill

J. P. Brower came to Fayetteville in 1904 from Northfield, Ohio, son of Alonzo James and Miriam Anata Stanford Brower. He married Fayetteville's Edith Adams-Davies, whose father was the Rev. Samuel Wilson Davies. In 1907, Mr. Brower established the Brower Walnut Veneer and Lumber Company from the burnt remnants of the Pitkin & Mayes facility at Fayette Junction. Brower's operation was ranked among the largest such concerns in the nation. Campbell's history relates that:

> J. P. Brower began cutting walnut lumber into dimension timbers for export. He soon saw that Northwest Arkansas had a magnificent walnut timber. Knowing the value of American Walnut when cut into veneering, he put machinery for doing this in 1913. With small beginning, he worked what was within short distances. When the World War came on he was requisitioned to make gunstocks for all his utmost capacity would stand. He went into the market at every station for 50 miles around Fayetteville and had thousands of logs on station yards when the armistice was signed. Suddenly there was no more need for gunstocks. He faced ruin. But instead of backing out he plunged into the veneering game in a big way, kept his plant running full and extra time, receiving one order for 12 cars of veneering from a Chicago factory. Those logs are long since gone and for 50 miles they are coming to him now [1928] by truckloads as well as carlots. He is also manufacturing strawberry baskets and grape baskets from cull veneering, and employs a large group of skilled labor.[12]

Anne Johnson Prichard of Fayetteville remembers that the

---

[12] Campbell

operations of Brower Veneer included a whistle that could be heard for miles signaling the noon hour. She reminisced that her father observed that "when the whistle sounded, the mules wouldn't go another step." Her family farm south of Fayetteville includes a barn whose support posts are solid walnut cores from the mill, remainders when the machinery had whirled off veneer down to the minimum diameter.

J. P Brower served as senior warden for the Episcopal Church and as a member of the founding board responsible for the establishment of the Fayetteville County Club at its current location on South Mountain. In 1909, he drove a Flanders roadster and in 1919, he owned a Willys Knight. He died September 7, 1934, at his residence of 207 N. College, with Alexander McCartney and J. H. Phipps among his honorary pallbearers. The company continued, however. Brower Veneer was still in operation at Fayette Junction in 1951.

E. A. Budd

E. A. Budd was a talented young transplant from Illinois who traded in fence posts cut from the hardwood forest. Settlement westward tamed the prairie and wild lands with fence, mostly regions where trees for fence posts were

As Robert Winn wrote in his book *Winslow: Top of the Ozarks*, "[Budd] had a large office with a staff of a dozen young ladies mailing out advertising for fence posts. He shipped out uncounted numbers of fence posts to western states. He also carried a complete line of clothing, shoes, feed, hardware, furniture, and groceries. Postcard image, author's possession.

hard to find. Railcar loads of Budd's posts shipped out from points along the Frisco track in south Washington County, especially from Winslow where the E. A. Budd Post Company Department Store offered "office, dry goods, shoes, clothing, furniture, groceries, hardware, flour & feed" in a fancy two-story building just east of the tracks. Locals complained about the mountainous stacks of posts in the midst of their "downtown." Budd had a general merchandise store in Chester and other outlying communities along the railroad, but most of his riches were invested in Fayetteville. He and his brother Arthur built a complex of businesses on the Fayetteville Square including Budd's Department Store, the Royal Theater, the Royal Café, and the Royal Barber Shop, all located in a strip along the south side of the square with the address of 19 ½ W. Mountain. The Budds built homes at 214 S. Block and 205 W. Rock, with the Rock Street house still standing as a showcase of fine hardwood carpentry.

At Fayette Junction, a ten-foot wide concrete drive and a 635' "Pro." track were built to serve Budd Post and Hardwood Company, the map lines crossing into an area also shown as the Sligo Wagon Wood Company mill. It is not clear from the 1916 Frisco map how Budd's operation fit into the sequence of other Fayette Junction milling operations. He may have simply used Fayette Junction as a checkpoint for posts pre-cut at their origin. The 1930 Sanborn Fire Insurance maps are the only Sanborn record naming Budd operations, and they show nothing of Budd at Fayette Junction. Instead, they show that by 1930 Budd had an office at 527 South Government-Cemetery Avenue, with the mill lying west of his office along the Frisco spur which ran parallel to Wall Street (6th Street).

Map notations describe his business as "Budd Posts Hardwood Company, manufacturers of wagon wood parts." The buildings

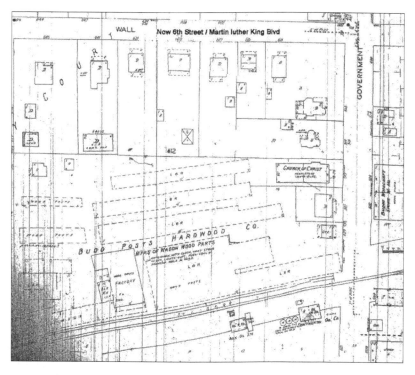

Budd Posts on S. Government Avenue, 1930. South Hill bounds the left side of this view, marked as "unpaved."

are labeled "wood posts factory." "Budds Woodcraft Spoke Warehouse" was across the street at 520-522 S. Government. Budd's businesses on the square were destroyed by fire on January 15, 1940, but he was able to rebuild; the 1947 directory lists Budd's mill at 521 (Cemetery) Government, his Post and Hardware Company at 9 W. Mountain, and Budd's Department Store "dry goods" also at 9 W. Mountain.[13]

End of the Line

All the timber from points east and south came through Fayette Junction, where railroad crews tended the engines, hooked up or dropped off cars on the sidings, threw appropriate switches, and

---

[13] More about E. A. Budd's life is found in *Rex Perkins: A Biography*, by this author.

communicated by telegraph, written messages, and word of mouth with various station agents about activities along the tracks. Serving as conductor along the early St. Paul line required a special breed of man, epitomized by the fabled "Irish" John Mulrenin who took on the job after three predecessors had quit in quick succession. For the next thirty years he handled the passengers of the St. Paul line, not just families and businessmen, but backwoods lumberjacks and diamond-jeweled card sharks. He became skilled in quick decisions such as cutting short the Pettigrew switching chores to leave drunks stranded at the depot.

~~~

The Fayette Junction tracks formed a "Y", with the southern "wye" used for "storage" and the northern for "industry". Where the northern "wye" joined the main track near the northernmost point of present-day Vale Avenue, there was a gravel platform, water tank, and depot, although there was never a passenger depot at Fayette Junction. Inside the "Y," Frisco built mechanical department buildings including a shop and storeroom, an 813 foot long "cinder pit" track, and a 416 foot long "depress" track, according to the 1916 Frisco map. At the southern end of the "Y" was a coal chute track, a coaling plant, boiler room, and a sand house.

To reach Fayette Junction from the Fayetteville Square, a traveler journeyed west on Center or Mountain Street before turning south on School or West. At the bottom of the hill, the road (originally called Bridge Street, later Prairie Street) turned west to cross a small creek and then south along Government (Cemetery) Road in an area known as Quicktown which served as a natural commerce point at a 'Y' intersection of the road south to the government cemetery and the road west that originally went to Cane Hill. Later this road was called the Prairie Grove Road or Wall Street,

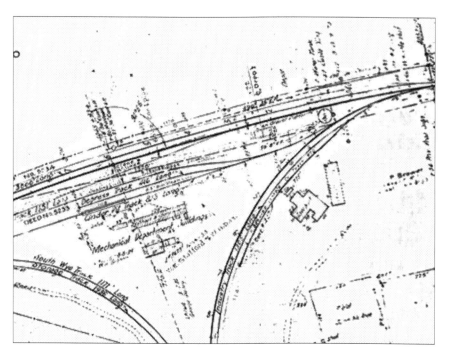

Fayette Junction 'wye' map, courtesy Engineering Department, City of Fayetteville

and still later 6th Street, then Martin Luther King Boulevard. Government Street was renamed Leroy Pond Road in 2020.

The road south to the National Cemetery turned west 11th Street, crossed over another small creek then turned onto South Duncan for about three blocks to the intersection of Town Street (now named 15th Street). After another block or so westward on 15th, a traveler would turn south onto Brooks Avenue, angling southwest for about three blocks.

But as the cemetery grew and blocked this route, the road changed so that by 1900 a traveler headed south to Fayette Junction would turn off Government onto Prairie Grove Road for two blocks west before turning south down Hill Street to intersect with 11th Street and rejoin the old Butterfield route. A block-long jog westward on

At the crossing of Town Creek, the road became South Garland,

and after about three blocks, Fayette Junction lay just ahead and to the right. The road (South Garland) passed the Sligo mill, immediately crossed the St. Paul line tracks, and turned west (right) onto Cato Springs Road which as late as 1908 did not connect eastward (left) with the more modern dominant southbound roadway South School Street (Hwy 71 B). This connection was hindered by a large streambed and swampy area. Cato Springs Road ran west about six blocks then south through the countryside toward Hog Eye, Strickler, and Fort Smith.

~~~

Fayette Junction and its industry became the center of a growing Fayetteville suburb, the farthest-flung (for its day) concentration of commerce and residences outside a central cluster around the Fayetteville square. Parksdale addition, a 1906 development project of J. A. Parks with J. T. Eason and Company as his agents, contained 212 lots of various sizes from Town Street (15th St.) on the north, along Brooks on the west, to the St. Paul tracks on the south, and both sides of Duncan along the east. Other streets laid out within this development were named after Fayetteville founders Walker, Boone, Pettigrew, Stirman, and Price, and six acres were set aside for a park now named Greathouse Park. The 1955 construction of the Levi Strauss plant overtook the lots south of the park and most of those along Pettigrew Street. Most lots were 25 feet wide ranging in depth from 120 feet up to 200 feet.

The smaller size was available for $10 and provided a place for parking a covered wagon or pitching a tent, or building a rough cabin, plus room for a vegetable garden. Evidence of the borderline financial existence of many Parksdale residents is found in the 1938 real estate tax records, which show that during this Depression period fully one half of the properties had been placed in the hands of the state government for failure to pay taxes

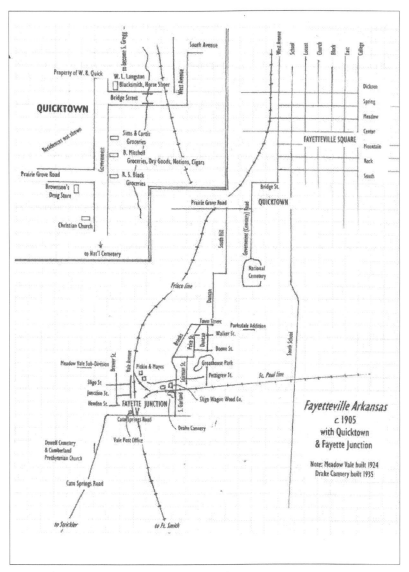

Map by author

(22 out of 44). One lot, at the intersection of Town (15th) and Brooks, was assigned to the Methodist Episcopal Church, probably under the influence of circuit-riding preacher O. H. Tucker, who owned all twenty lots across Brooks Street in Block 2. Today in driving through this neighborhood, one can spot several occupied dwellings which probably date to 1906 or earlier.

Meadow Vale subdivision, lying immediately west of the main Frisco line and north of Cato Springs Road, was added to Fayetteville in 1924. Lots ranged in size from 30'x150' up to 300'x450'. Streets were named Hendon, Brower, Sligo, Junction, and Vale, with those along Vale facing the rail bed. Appraised values of these properties ranged from $10 up to $350 in the 1926 tax records. A strip through the middle of Meadow Vale was razed for the 1999 expansion of Razorback Road to connect with Interstate 49. A few original structures remain occupied.

No doubt some of the workers employed by Sligo lived in these neighborhoods and raised their families here. Various sources mention 30 up to 85 employees for the company; the aforementioned 1925 photograph of Sligo Wagon Wood Company workers shows 38 men, most in overalls, lined up on the west side of the main building. J. P. Brower and his Brower Veneer Company also employed men in Fayette Junction operations, and railroad employees who serviced the line to St. Paul and the main Frisco line may have lived in Parksdale and Meadow Vale.

The Vale Post Office, whose mail was processed through Fayetteville, was established August 27, 1901 and was located at the northwest corner of Vale and Cato Springs Road intersection. Ed Moran, born at Fayette Junction in 1912, recalled a store at the location of the post office: "The Steven Reed family ran the post office and the store and lived upstairs." A 1904 grocery at Fayette Junction, probably at the same location, was "Bentley and Keeler."

The Fayette Junction telegraph office began operations in 1915, believed housed in the Fayette Junction depot, approximately 1800 S. Vale. Washington County Schoolhouse #157 was located about a half mile south and west of the post office along Cato Springs Road, the nearest such facility in 1908. A Cumberland Presbyterian Church sat across the road from the school on land owned by H. J.

Dowell, adjacent to the present-day Dowell Cemetery at the intersection of Cato Springs Road and Interstate 49.

Wye Operations

The Frisco Fayette Junction Roundhouse was listed in the 1932 Fayetteville directory with a telephone number of 641 under "Railroads" in the Yellow Pages. The Personal Data Book of the Division Superintendent for the Ft. Smith station reported the Fayette Junction population that year was fifty, but it is not clear what area he considered "Fayette Junction." Three years later, Superintendent S. T. Cantrell inventoried the 75 steam engines and other assets of the division. The oldest engine of the bunch, a "ten-wheeler" No. 488 Baldwin 1910, was in mixed service on the St. Paul to Bentonville line.

Also in use to St. Paul was another oil-burner 4-6-0, No. 552 Pittsburgh 1901. Cantrell reported the following locomotive assignments to Fayette Junction as of February 26, 1935. In the shop: #598, 4-6-0, oil, Dickson 1903. In storage: #648, 4-6-0, oil, Baldwin 1904; #750 4-6-0, oil, Baldwin 1902; #755, 4-6-0, oil, Baldwin 1902; #779 4-6-0, oil, Baldwin 1903; #3651 0-6-0, oil, Baldwin 1906; #3676 0-6-0, coal, Baldwin 1905#3695 0-6-0, coal, Baldwin 1906. Later observers remarked on the number of engines in storage as evidence of the "sorry state" of the railroads by 1935.

The November 19, 1905 train schedule from Fayetteville to Pettigrew left the Dickson Street station at 8:10 a.m., passed through Fayette Junction at 8:40 a.m., and arrived at Pettigrew at 11:50 a.m., with stops at Baldwin, Harris, Elkins, Durham, Thompson, Crosses, Delaney, Patrick, Combs, Brashears, St. Paul, and Dutton. After turning the engine on the roundhouse at Pettigrew, the train departed at 12:55 p.m., and arrived at Fayetteville at 4:15 p.m. In 1915, the train ran approximately fifteen minutes earlier, with the stop at Baldwin now named

"Leith." Return run arrived in Fayetteville at 3:30 p.m. The same schedule and stops were in place in 1927.

The Fayette Junction station force in 1932 included an agent-telegraph operator at work 6 a.m. until 3 p.m., with a stipend of $0.67 per day. Holidays the hours were 6:15 a.m. until 8:15 a.m. The schedule by 1931 for 'St. Paul Branch' showed a mixed train daily (passengers and freight), starting from Fayetteville at 7:45 a.m., arriving Pettigrew at 11a.m., leaving Pettigrew at 12:01 p.m. to return to Fayetteville, where it arrived at 3:10 p.m. All the intermediate stations were shown as flag stops except for Combs, where the train stopped at 9:54 a.m. on the outbound trip and 12:50 p.m. on the return trip, and St. Paul at 10:15 a.m. on the outbound trip and 12:30 p.m. on the return trip.

The fifty years from 1887 to 1937 had seen it all come and go through Fayette Junction. According to favored accounts, the last train to St. Paul ran July 30, 1937, "when 'Irish' Mulrenin had in his charge one wheezing locomotive, Mogul #345, and one empty, creaking old wooden coach" with a crate of two hound dogs as passengers. The logging boom had come to an end. The tracks were taken up some time after, but remained across south Fayetteville accommodating various manufacturers in the new Fayetteville industrial park (east of City Lake Road, south of Hwy 16 East) and the shipment of new and recycled metal to and from Ozark Steel Company on South School as late as the 1970s. Industrial activity dependent on the railway continued at Fayette Junction. Immediately following the termination of activities by Sligo Wagon Wood Company circa 1930, the enormous old mill building served as a convenient loading point for Hargis Canneries.

Tom Hargis

From the opening of the railroad through Fayetteville, local fruits and other produce began to enjoy a popular national demand. Made famous by an early and enthusiastic market for its delicious apples, Northwest Arkansas quickly expanded its food industry by producing dried and canned foods. By 1905 a Fayetteville cannery industry had sprung up for tomatoes, berries, and apples, although the majority of the region's canning business centered in Springdale.

Early Frisco express agents in Fayetteville were credited with helping farmers move crops of strawberries "and other small fruits by assisting them to find markets, building up the reputation of this place as a source of supply.... Fayetteville became such a great shipping point that through the fruit season an express car was often set out here for loading aside from the regular local train loadings."

At the site of Fayetteville's defunct Ozark Wagon plant at Arkansas Avenue and West Center, Appleby Brothers ran a "green-and-dried-apple" business plus a large cannery operation. In 1928 production exceeded 250 carloads of canned goods with plants located from Winslow up to Decatur in Benton County. Other cannery operations included Litteral Canning Company, whose building remains just west of the tracks at North Street.

At Fayette Junction, Tom Hargis operated Hargis Canneries as a brokerage for nearly thirty small canneries that dotted the remote hillsides and valleys of Washington and Madison Counties. At each local enterprise, his trucks dropped off empty cans and supplies and picked up canned lots of tomatoes, spinach, and green beans to be warehoused at the old Sligo mill. From there, train carloads would be packed off to distant grocery wholesalers, while local wholesalers received direct deliveries.

Hargis Cannery Company provided an important service for isolated family and community canning cooperatives which came

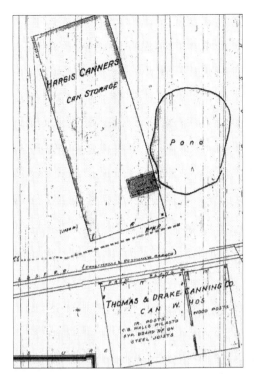

together to build and equip canning facilities. Unlike larger urban canning operations, rural canneries served by Hargis were whole families or small communities who worked to get their crops picked, hauled, washed, skinned, cooked and/or otherwise processed into cans. In a good season, if nature withheld late frost, cooperated with adequate rainfall, and sent only manageable waves of blister beetles, grasshoppers, cutworm, and stink bugs, the summer crops quickly processed and preserved in tin-plated steel cans would contribute sufficient income in support of the rural family's coming winter.

Tom Hargis (b. 1882 Marble, Madison County, Arkansas; d September 1981 Huntsville Mad Co) was the grandson of Pleasant Hargis, who came to Madison County from Tennessee in 1843. The family settled on Onion Creek where Pleasant's descendants remain. Pleasant's son Peter Columbus "Lum" Hargis was among the original founders of the First National Bank of Huntsville. William Thomas "Tom" Hargis carried on his father's tradition of ownership at the bank and pursued other enterprise as well. A half-block of native stone buildings on the southeast corner of Huntsville's town square bears the family name. Hargis was also the vice-president of Kelley Brothers Lumber Company of Huntsville, with its lumberyards in Fayetteville (605 W. Dickson) and three other towns. He was appointed by the governor as one of three men serving Northwest Arkansas in the establishment of vocational schools. He was partner in the Ford dealership in Huntsville, worked to merge and improve early banking operations in Madison County where he experienced at least one bank robbery (1912), and earned the respect of many in the region.

"Tom Hargis was a good man. If someone needed some money, Tom had it for you. He knew everyone, and he kept Madison County on its feet during the Depression. He built a cannery and gave people jobs when there weren't any." (Whittemore V I, p 65)

From the early 1930s until 1951, Tom Hargis saw to it that canned goods produced in rural areas were warehoused and shipped from the old Sligo mill building at Fayette Junction. Tom Hargis was the company president, his sister Mildred's husband James O. Witt Jr. was the vice-president, and Mildred was secretary-treasurer. Tom's canning interests included one or more facilities in New Mexico.

By 1936, the canning business was the dominant regional industry. At Fayette Junction, a new facility sprang up right across the tracks from Sligo and began its own railcar shipments of canned goods. The 1936 Sanborn maps document this enterprise as "Thomas and Drake Canning Company Warehouse," remarking that stated building dimensions had been taken "from plans." It was a state of the art facility: plans specified iron posts, concrete block pilaster, and gypsum board roof on steel joists. The Rev. Jake Drake and his son Ezra Drake joined with Rylan C. Thomas in this enterprise.

According to the 1939 city directory, "Drake and Hargis Cannery" was located at 605 W. Dickson. Crates of canned tomatoes, greens, and other produce from this cannery would have been warehoused at Fayette Junction. In 1947, the business was called

"Thomas and Drake Canning" and had offices at 19 East Center. Several Drakes may have been involved as a venture of the extended Drake family of Drake's Creek area, Madison County. It is not clear whether the Fayette Junction property built by Drake ever served as more than a storage facility. Drake's brother Bill and sister-in-law Vida operated a favored local café known first as "Bill Drake's Place,"[14] no doubt taking advantage of his brother's access to inexpensive local canned goods. At some point before 1951, Drake and Thomas was taken over by Hargis. Among the litter later found on the old Sligo mill's vast shadowy floor were cancelled checks of Drake Canning Company and Thomas and Drake Canning Company with dates in the 1950s.

Hargis and Drake canneries rode a wave of profitable commerce as Arkansas fruits and vegetables, especially tomatoes, captured a significant market share nationally. But by 1950, production and sales of tomato and strawberry crops comprised a mere one-fourth the volume it had enjoyed in 1930. Disease, economic forces, and stringent new sanitation regulations began to crush the local canning market.

The working class neighborhoods of Fayette Junction were fortunate to find jobs in a new facility built directly across South Garland east of the old Sligo mill. When the Levi Strauss plant opened in 1955, rows of sewing machines operated by scores of women occupied a vast workroom of over 40,000 square feet.

---

[14] Vida Drake continued the business after Bill's death. Frequent winner of awards for best plate lunch, "Ma Drake's" continued her café even after suffering a heart attack in the early 1990s. Her lunches included a meat, mashed potatoes with gravy, three vegetables, salad, and a roll for $3.75. Homemade pies rounded off the menu, usually available in apple, cherry, lemon, chocolate, coconut, and pecan. The café was first located at the northeast corner of Sixth and S. College, but later moved to 504 E. 15th Street. Drake's closed with her death in 1997.

Millions of pairs of Levi jeans were produced there. The Levi facility served as one of the best-paying Fayetteville factory employers until it closed in 1998 by which time globalization had undercut American labor.

As the canneries declined, rural family farms were encouraged into the chicken production business with production and marketing support offered by companies like Tyson's, which served as an "integrator." The same two decades that fruit and vegetable crops deteriorated saw a leap in chicken production from about 250,000 in 1930 to 10 million in 1950. From 1951 until 1962, Hargis and other partners (Rogers and Witt Hatchery Incorporated, Rogers and Witt Milling Company (feed), and Arkansas Farmers Hatchery) used the Sligo building as a chicken hatchery. Fertile eggs were laid out in drawers made of hardware cloth, so that warm air could circulate to foster even hatching. Tall "chests" holding two vertical rows of egg drawers rolled on steel wheels for ease of processing and cleaning. Chicks were delivered to farmers who would then raise them to fryer age. Across the tracks in the old Drake buildings were Gallus Hatchery and an early J. B. Hunt rice hull chicken litter operation. The day for this industry would also pass; the late 50s and early 60s saw the hatchery business taken out of the hands of independent, small producers like Hargis and Rogers as they were subsumed by Tyson and other corporate giants.

Lumber Warehousing Returns to Sligo Mill Building

Around 1962, the Sligo mill building came back around to a familiar use, its concrete floors again bearing up under loads of new lumber. This time, however, the lumber was not oak and hickory from nearby mountainsides, but pine from south Arkansas and redwood from the West Coast. Starting in 1966 and for the next ten years, Reserve Supply Lumber (Frank Jones of

Carthage, Missouri) used the Sligo building in wholesaling to lumber yards in the region. In those days, lumber was loaded loose into railcars and shipped out from the Pacific Northwest, where the timber boom had hit its peak. Company representatives would call lumber yard owners to announce what was coming on the train. Lumber yard owners would place their orders, so that when the railcar was opened on the track beside the warehouse, teams of men unloading the jammed unbundled lumber could stack the materials directly onto delivery trucks. Unsold remnants would be stored in the Sligo mill building.

Ownership of the Sligo mill property passed through Hargis-Witt family descendants to City Lumber Company. After the mid-1970s, City Lumber Company used the building for storage of lumber and other supplies. Two newer storage sheds were built in the same location as Sligo's early side-track warehouses where now-bundled lumber could be kept until needed at the lumber yard. Slowly, the mill building deteriorated. Thieves made midnight raids. Finally, in the early 1990s, City Lumber abandoned the warehouse. In the mid-1990s, after 100 years of use, Burlington Northern Railroad sold off all the Fayette Junction land except the right-of-way along the remaining tracks.

The neighborhood struggled in a continuing decline until the late 1990s, when Razorback Road was extended south from 15th Street, punching through the old Meadow Vale neighborhood to connect with Cato Springs Road and Interstate 49. The new road makes a convenient link between the newly completed four-lane highway and University of Arkansas sports facilities. Investors have constructed a large warehouse complex just north of the Sligo property, Fayetteville Warehouse Company. In 2002, a new apartment complex opened south of the junction, at the corner of Garland and Cato Springs Road. Red Spot LLC, a concrete company, loads trucks out of its mixing plant built in the center of the "Y".

Now under ownership of a local construction company, three rusting Brower Veneer Company buildings are surrounded by metal salvage and rank vegetation. Across Town Creek to the north of Brower is University of Arkansas land which faces the former Campbell Soup plant at 15th street on its north side and has been developed as parking and services hook-up for recreational vehicles which swarm over Fayetteville at times of University sports events. The City of Fayetteville has made fits and starts toward constructing a hiking/biking trail along the abandoned portion of the old St. Paul rail bed across south Fayetteville, starting eastward from the Sligo mill.

Before its demolition in May 2004, the cavernous old Sligo/Hargis/City Lumber warehouse sat empty, its vast roof sagging in spots where the post and beam framing had started to fail after one hundred years of termites, weather, and gravity. Long ago, its owners slathered tar over the sheet metal roof to stave off rust and leaks, so that the massive mottled black surface resembled a half-acre of burnt earth. At either end of the building's two-hundred-fifteen-foot length stood tall double doors set in massive frames of upright oak posts. Scattered papers and odd bits of lumber littered the dark expanse inside; two old tables too long and heavy to lift sat waiting for the next job, most recently serving the homeless person who had left an uncased pillow on the scarred surface.

Inside the building in its southeast corner was the 18' x 30' brick structure that housed the fiery steam boilers, oil stains still splotched black on its walls. The handmade orange-red brick was painted white at some early point, later cluttered with graffiti. Two small windows looked east in the brick room's only remaining exterior wall so that from the road as one stared at the old warehouse, one saw the windows in a short section of faded brick wall, incongruous in the overall sheet-iron gray length of the building. A massive elm had buried its roots under the brick wall corner, heaving up the native stone foundation.

The perimeter of the huge mill building's concrete floor—the only remainder now of its long life—is sprigged with trees young and old, the grounds nearby crawling with honeysuckle and thunder briar. In the half-acre of land between the building and Garland Avenue nestles a tiny pool of water skirted by willows and cattails, a fragment of the ponds built long ago to feed the steam boilers that powered the saws and planers housed inside.

Sources for History of Fayette Junction

Allen, Desmond Walls, *Arkansas School Land Sales 1883-1997.* Arkansas Research: Conway

Arkansas Railroader newsletter

Campbell, W. C. *One Hundred Years of Fayetteville*; Washington County Historical Society

Cook, Don, and Tom Maringer, *Postal History of Washington County, Arkansas*

Fayetteville Democrat Weekly June 22, 1888

Flashback – several editions

Frisco Lines Central Division, Ft. Smith, Sub-Division Yard Plat 1916 map, Offices of Fayetteville City Engineer

Genealogy Section of Fayetteville Public Library

Harnish Doctoral Dissertation, Special Collections, University of Arkansas Fayetteville

History of Benton, Washington, Carroll, Madison, Crawford, Franklin, and Sebastian County, Arkansas. Chicago: The Goodspeed Publishing Company 1889

History of Washington County 1989; Shiloh Museum, Springdale Arkansas

Hull, Clifton E. "When the Steam Cars Finally Came to Old St. Paul," *Arkansas Gazette* March 28, 1971.

Rice, Phyllis "Moran recalls old Fayette Junction," *Northwest Arkansas Times* Apr 11, 1988: Fayetteville

Sanborn Fire Insurance Maps, University of Arkansas Fayetteville

Shiloh Museum, vertical files

Washington County Archives

Western Historical Manuscript Collection (online), University of Missouri, Rolla

Whittemore, Carol et al, *Fading Memories: A history of the lives and times of Madison County people* Vol. I; 1989

Winn, Robert G., "Timber" *Washington County Observer* March 25, 1982

Special Thanks to:

Anne Johnson Prichard and the entire staff at Special Collections, University of Arkansas Fayetteville

Peggy Hackler and the entire staff at the Genealogy Section of the Fayetteville Public Library

Rob and Nancy Witt Lewis

Shiloh Museum

Washington County Archives

Quicktown: Here then gone

A relic of early Fayetteville

Quicktown was the name of a small Fayetteville neighborhood that rose and fell in less than two decades between 1883 and the early 1900s. It lay southwest of the Fayetteville Square along Prairie Street (previously Bridge Street) and Government Avenue (previously Cemetery Road). Named after the Quick family and properties owned by James W. Quick and his son William R. Quick, the neighborhood offered a place of commerce outside the town square more easily accessible for heavy wagons than the Square, which sat on a steep hill. During its prime, Quicktown hosted residences and businesses offering groceries, supplies, blacksmithing, and other necessities of the day.

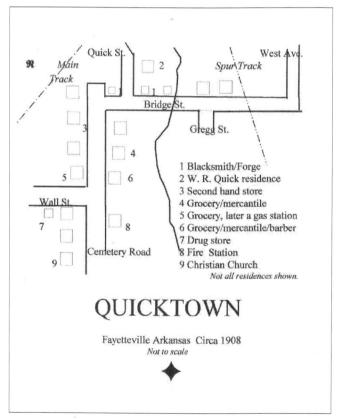

Quicktown grew up around an early road that led south and west out of town. The original road angled down from the town square across unsettled land where it flattened at the bottom of the hill, roughly following the end of West Avenue. Passage over the spring-fed creek required a bridge, thus setting a specific route for the roadway. Beyond the creek, the road branched into two routes, one that led west toward Prairie Grove (Wall Street on the map) and one that led south to the national cemetery and beyond.

This path south had been "surveyed and supervised" by the United States Army in 1835 as part of the first military road from St. Louis to Ft. Smith, and followed earlier Native American (Osage) hunting trails. The area's early settlers obtained goods mostly from the west at Cane Hill, Evansville, and Ft. Gibson, or through the much more arduous journey over the mountains to Fort Smith. Generally, goods traveled up the Arkansas River past Fort Smith to Fort Gibson, which allowed supply wagons to come into the area from Indian Territory (Oklahoma) and avoid the mountains.

Bridge Street was part of the route used by the Butterfield Stage in the late 1850s and by armies of both the North and the South during the Civil War. After the war, the established roadway continued to support mounted riders and wagon traffic, although the arrival of the railroad in 1881 and a sudden increase in housing and commercial activity hardened the route. Set within a narrow low lying area between the main railroad tracks and the more eastern spur track which served feed suppliers, millers, and stockyards, the area of Quicktown took shape.

In the 1904 Fayetteville City Directory, Bridge Street's location was described as "Quicktown, begins at Cemetery Road thence east to south West Street." Regular crossing of this year-round creek would have required a bridge early in Fayetteville's existence, and the importance of the bridge is reflected in the original naming of the street. Even as late as the early 20th century, this thoroughfare remained the primary south and west route into and out of town because it was the least steep passage down from the town square.

At its earliest known existence, Quicktown began where West Avenue hits Prairie Street just south of Fayetteville's Blair Public Library. The "town" then spread westward along both sides of Bridge/Prairie Street. Bridge Street did not cut eastward from West Avenue as Prairie does today; Barker & Stephenson's brick yard occupied this area as early as 1868 where a fine red-clay embankment supported their lucrative business of making bricks for the growing town.

The first block of Bridge/Prairie crossed the spur railroad track, the old rail bed of which is now Fayetteville's multi-use Frisco Trail. The next block crossed the creek, now named Tanglewood Branch. In another half block, the road turned south for a block and then split. The path continuing south became Cemetery Road (now Government Avenue) for three blocks to the government cemetery. The road that turned west was named "Wall Street" but has since become 6th Street and Martin Luther King Boulevard. At that time, Wall Street did not venture further east than Cemetery Road because of the morass of swampy land draining the creek.

Wall Street was the road to Prairie Grove, Evansville, and other points west as it remains today. Due to growth of the cemetery, by around 1900 Cemetery Road dead-ended at the cemetery and persons wishing to travel further south detoured a few blocks along Wall Street before turning south on South Hill Street to reach Fayette Junction. From there, the old Butterfield road carried travelers on a tenuous journey through Hogeye, Strickler, and over the mountains to Fort Smith.

Within the Quicktown area, by the late 1800s two local streets adjoined Bridge Street in its short length, one to the north which was named Quick and one to the south, named Gregg. In the 1904 directory, the route of Quick Street (which now is also named

Gregg) was described as being from "Bridge north to railroad" — about one block. It connected to the main railroad tracks at the corner now occupied by the Key Architecture building but did not continue north beyond that point. A dirt lane trekked further northward parallel to the tracks and this later became the Prairie-to-Center section of Gregg Street. The 1908 Fayetteville City Map shows a dotted line running north from Bridge to Center Street along the current mostly-creekside route of South Gregg.

While today much of this neighborhood rests under a canopy of tall trees, in the late 1800s the area would have been largely cleared. The difficult work of removing trees by hand saw and ax increased property values significantly. Old growth trees were cut along the rail beds to make way for the main track and spur track, and also along the creek bottom running between the two tracks to allow for homes and household gardens in this small valley. The creek would have been a year-round water supply as it was (and is) fed by a large spring rising near the Walton Arts Center at Spring Street. Marshy land alongside the creek was drained and the waterway channelized to allow for optimum land usage.

During Quicktown's brief heyday, several residences and businesses occupied street frontage along Bridge and two or three blocks south down Cemetery Road. Goodspeed's 1889 history provides the first business listing for the area, naming James W. Quick as a blacksmith. The location of his forge, as marked on the attached map, is now a vacant lot. Unfortunately no other record exists for Quicktown business activity that is contemporary to its prime years except a reference by William Campbell in his 1928 *100 Years of Fayetteville*. He writes that all the town's stores surrounded the Fayetteville square until "they began to spring up in the nineties... down by the old White mill, out the Mt. Comfort road, down in "Quicktown." (p 13)

The Quicks' land ownership at the area named "Quicktown" lasted about two decades, but like the very definition of the word "quick," Quicktown came and went in even less time. By the time of the 1908 city map, Quick Street was not shown and Bridge Street had become Prairie Street. James' land ownership at Quicktown peaked around 1890, and after the untimely deaths of two adult children in 1891 and 1893, he sold off his remaining properties there. In 1906, he repurchased some of this property. His son William retained selected Quicktown property ownership at least through 1908.

The 1900 census for Fayetteville is the next record of Quicktown's activity. It lists James W. Quick's blacksmith business. A few doors down from the blacksmith operation, the 1900 census finds his son William working as a merchant. The 1900 neighborhood hosted residences and businesses including a second hand store, machine shop, grocer/mercantile, barber, drug store, and probably other enterprise as well. No street addresses were given for these establishments and it can only be assumed that, like James Quick's forge, they existed for roughly a decade before the census taker arrived. (The 1890 federal census was lost in fire.)

The 1904 Fayetteville City Directory listed residents living on Quick Street, including laborer John Perry and his daughter Addie, farmer Joseph Wilson (stepson of James Quick), and J. H. and Edgar Fritts, teamsters. Will Quick is listed as a grocery merchant living on "Quick Street adjacent to Bridge." In the neighborhood of Bridge, Quick, Gregg, Cemetery, and the corner of Wall Street, the 1904 directory lists 48 individuals residing in 32 households or rooms. The working class occupants of these quarters included building tradesmen (stone cutter, stonemason, molder, carpenter, wood worker), railroad employees, merchants (grocers, barber), laborers, teamsters, farmers, firemen, a couple of retirees, and that ubiquitous Fayetteville resident, University of Arkansas students.

The 1908 Fayetteville City Map shows W. L. Langston, Blacksmith, in the old James Quick location. The map also shows a grocer with warehouse, drug store, church, and fire department arrayed mostly along Cemetery Road. W. R. Quick's residence is shown in the location described in the 1904 directory, but the map makes no mention of his occupation as "merchant."

The Quicks for whom Quicktown was named did not own land in Fayetteville until 1883, but the family had been in and out of the area since before the Civil War. James W. Quick was born January 3, 1839, in Edgar County, Illinois. He was in Polk County, Missouri by 1859, when he married Mary Hurt. (Polk County lies about 30 miles north of Springfield.) Their first child was born in 1860 in Sebastian County, Arkansas, and the second child in 1861 in Scott County, Arkansas. Perhaps the Kansas-Missouri violence preceding the Civil War caused the young family to seek safer territory, or perhaps they were simply looking for better economic opportunity. Between 1864 and 1873 five more children were born, all in Polk County, Missouri. The 1880 census finds James, Mary, and family in Sebastian County, Arkansas, with five children attending school.

By March 26, 1883, James Quick and family were in Washington County at which time he filed a military pension claim with the assistance of the county clerk's office. The claim records show that he enlisted June 16, 1863, and was discharged April 3, 1865. He served as farrier (horseshoer) for Company E, 1st Arkansas Cavalry Volunteers, United States. He reported no Confederate service and no hospitalization. He fought at the Battle of Fayetteville (Tomahawk Bluff) and served with Captains Galloway and King,

Lieutenant Kincaid, and Sergeant Dotherty. He named comrades George Hoyle and James Irby, and described himself as 5 feet 11 inches with dark complexion, gray eyes, and dark hair. He was a member and officer of Travis Post No. 19 Grand Army of the Republic, Fayetteville. (Goodspeed p 251)

As the "founder" of Quicktown, James W. Quick bought his first property in Washington County August 25, 1883, a 0.16 acre outlot in the area soon to be called Quicktown, for which he paid $20. Over the next three decades he was able to purchase over 15 parcels of land in Washington County including acreage or lots at Greathouse Springs, Fayette Junction, Prairie Grove, and other areas of the county. He sold seven lots and financed three mortgages between 1885 and 1889; seven lots and two mortgages between 1890 and 1899; and six lots between 1900 and 1910. Real estate taxes paid by James between 1884 and 1894 covered four properties in Quicktown: Block 16 Township 16, Range 30 in the Southeast portion of the Southwest Quarter, and the Southwest portion of the Southeast Quarter. In 1884, he owned two parcels there for a total of 1.25 acres.

By 1885, Mr. Quick was paying taxes on 2.91 acres in the same area. These properties increased in value from $350 in 1884 to $600 in 1887, probably due to the addition of buildings. By 1889, he owned two additional parcels, for a total of 3.7 acres valued at $875. Between 1892 and 1893, his holdings were reduced to 1.66 acres with a value of $300, and 1894 was his last year shown in real estate tax records for the Quicktown area. However, two of his Quicktown lots were sold that year to James Cowen, and in 1901 James' second wife Celia re-bought the two lots from James Cowan, who is believed to have been Celia's father. In October 1906, Celia sold those lots back to James Quick in spite of their pending divorce.

James' son William R. Quick, the other Quick who owned land at Quicktown, also bought, sold, and mortgaged properties in Washington County, although not as many as his father. On the 1908 map, W. R. Quick was shown as owner of a large parcel of property on either side of Quick Street fronting Bridge, at which time he was 35 and had a wife Clara Elizabeth (Kessler) and an eight-year-old daughter Annie. A large two-story house torn down in the early 1990s which occupied the corner lot north of Bridge (Prairie) and east of Quick (S. Gregg) was likely the W. R. Quick residence. A slight knoll marks its former location.

County records show William purchased a total of five parcels of land, the first from his father in 1891 (Fayette Junction area) and several hundred acres in the Hazel Valley area. Will is not found in the 1910 census, but in 1920 he was working as an auctioneer in "general practice" and residing in Prairie Grove along with his wife Clara and three additional children. At the time of James' death in 1926, Will was named in the will to receive some money and a share of James' properties, while several lots of James' Prairie Grove property were left to Will's daughter Annie (then married to A. L. Harris). Clara filed for divorce in 1927, at which point William was nowhere to be found, and she ended up with custody of their remaining minor child William and eleven parcels of Prairie Grove real estate. No subsequent records are found for William R. Quick.

William was the last child of James' marriage to Mary Hurt (or Hunt), who died in Fayetteville September 30, 1886 when William was 13. Two older siblings died in Fayetteville, George M. in 1891 (age 22), and Nancy J. in 1893 (age 29), while John H.(age 17-19) died in Sebastian County between 1878 and 1880. James had seven children by his first wife Mary, and six more by his third wife Celia (Cecilia) Ann Cowen Wilson, whom he married at Black

Jack, Indian Territory, in 1888. In 1893, he gave his son William his power of attorney and moved to Indian Territory, where he obtained more land.

James pursued several legal actions in Fayetteville, including successful suits against parties who failed to pay for lots purchased from him at Quicktown. Emma and W. W. Harrison paid only $8.60 toward a mortgage of $396 at 10% interest with Moore and Gallihar/Gollaher as security and paid out through McIlroy and Co., bankers. (A "Hall & Gallagher Addition" appeared on city plats halfway between Prairie and Center Street, at the jog in South Gregg.) This property was sold at public auction in 1894. Another property deal involving L. W. Martin (also named were W. F. Winger, Annie Winger, Lester Lollar, and A. L. Trent) came before the court in 1916, with nothing being paid in two years on a vendor's lien of $750 at 6% interest. Quick bought back this parcel at public auction for $900.55.

By the time of the 1920 Fayetteville City Directory, no Quicks are listed, and there is no reference to Quicktown. However, Quicktown as a place lingered in Fayetteville's collective memory. Business locations can't be specifically tracked earlier than 1920, since the earliest surviving city directory (1904) gave only street names but not addresses. The next surviving issues are 1920, then 1929, 1935, 1939, and 1947. Quicktown businesses listed in these five directories include:

- Site of recently closed American Milling (500 Prairie) hosted the Owen C. Herr garage in 1929, O. K. Garage in 1935, Ozark Coal Company and Wilkinson Hatchery in 1939, and Wilkinson Hatchery & Milling in 1947. That location now populated by two-story town houses.

- The old "skateboard place" (505 Prairie) was Standard Oil Company in 1935, Standard Esso Oil Company in 1939, and Standard Oil Company Bulk Plant in 1947. In 2020, the spot was converted to an outdoor live music/food truck venue.
- The following sites have been subsumed by a new (2017) Walmart Neighborhood Market along the west frontage of Government:
    - ❖ Campbell 66 Express Inc. 1947 (343 Government, also known to have occupied 400-402),
    - ❖ A second hand store shown on the 1908 map, Henry Barnes Cabinet Shop 1935 and 1939 (417 Government),
    - ❖ George W. Widner grocery (423 Government),
    - ❖ Algie Moore grocery 1904 – 1920 then W. Lee Moore filling station and grocery 1929 - 1947 (425 Government). The Moore grocery/filling station may have been on the corner of 6th later owned by Fred Hannah for a boat sales concern in the late 1950s
- R. S. Black groceries, Sims & Curtis groceries, and B. Mitchell groceries, notions, dry goods, cigars (1904) were all located along the east side of Cemetery Road north of 6th, but were not identified with street numbers. B. Mitchell operation is the most likely candidate to have been the predecessor at Hammontree's 1920 site;
- D. E. Hammontree dry goods, feed & flour, hardware, groceries, and general merchandise 1920 (412 Cemetery), 2020 site of food trucks;
- G. F. Puterbaugh grocery (1920) supplanted either R. S. Black or Sims & Curtis at 428 Cemetery, which then became Rich Mercantile (Edw. H. Rich) by 1929 and then Thomas J. Jefferson,

Barber, from 1939 through 1947. This building remained through 2020 as the home of Heartwood Gallery art collective and Heartwood Creations cabinet shop.

- Chas. C. Smith filling station (1929) then T. K. Smith filling station (1935) occupied 430 Cemetery, a location not now identified. May have been site now facing 6th Street at corner of Government or may have been lost when 6th Street was extended east from Cemetery to connect with south School Avenue. Also lost with the street extension was a fire station.

Three structures of early construction remain standing along the east side of the 400 block of Government. Evidence of their age may be noted in their native stone foundations set down without poured footings, pine flooring, construction materials such as lathe board roof decking with shake shingles, and a small central core building later expanded with added sections.

Businesses located along Cemetery to the south of Cemetery/6th Street included Marland Oil, later Continental Oil; B & M Cabinet Company, Budd Post & Hardwood Mill; Red Star Spoke Company, later Miller Hardwood Company, Broyles planing mill and then Fayetteville Iron & Metal. These locations were outside the immediate area originally referred to as Quicktown, as were businesses located on Prairie Street east of West Avenue and the original Quicktown which developed when the roadway was extended eastward to connect with south School Avenue. These Prairie Street businesses included:

- 421 – Southwest Oil 1929, Thomas J. Jefferson barber 1935
- 422 – James W. Hall grocery 1929
- 423 – McCoy Gas Company 1929, Price Oil Company Service Station and McCoy Coal Company 1935, Hanshew Coal Company and Howard wood yard 1939, Arkansas Motor

Freight Lines Inc. 1947

- 434 – Bailey feeds, Black Diamond Coal Company and Fred Lester barber 1939, Nickell Hatchery and Andrew Mhoon barber 1947

Following the Civil War and the arrival of the railroad through Fayetteville, Cane Hill and other early commercial centers faded in importance and Fayetteville became the dominant regional community. Travelers along the early road out of town would have frequented any tavern or mercantile in Quicktown, sought out horseshoeing and other blacksmith services, and visited specialized enterprises such as a drug store, which until the early 1900s could dispense various patent medicines including compounds containing opium, cocaine, and alcohol.

Quicktown served as a convenient location for various shopping needs. Neighborhood residents would have frequented the businesses for groceries and other supplies or services and continued to do so for several decades until motorized transportation and re-routing of primary traffic corridors marginalized the area and left its businesses without adequate patronage. Land records through the 1920s and '30s show several properties endured repeated mortgages and forfeiture for back taxes. Quicktown's residential fortunes have not improved markedly since that time.

Fayetteville's Quicktown was not the only locale thusly named. Charles Sanders Peirce, considered by many as one of America's foremost intellects, purchased a Pennsylvania property on the Delaware River in the late 1880s called Quicktown (after its founder John Quick) which he continued to call Quicktown for many years before later changing the name to "Arisbe." Lackawanna County, Pennsylvania also hosts a Quicktown, and other Pennsylvania "Quick" places may have existed because the state was a settlement area for many early colonist Quicks who began migrating westward from New York and New Jersey. A present-day subdivision in South Carolina is named Quicktown, and Laurel Hill, North Carolina, has a Quicktown Road. There was a Quick City in Missouri (not known to be associated with the James Quick family) and another in Indiana, both now ghost towns. Likely all these places and many others now forgotten mark the journey of people named Quick.

Why Quick more than other surnames stands out as a notable location name may have more to do with the common meaning of the word. Many towns are named after founders, so the use of a surname isn't that unusual for settlements. But the meaning of "quick" as "alive," "alert," "easily angered," "hasty," or "fast" adds interest as well as a touch of humor to a location's description, and probably increased the likelihood of such a name being adopted—especially if one or more of the common definitions also applied to the personality of the Quicks in residence. Even today, the name of Quicktown rolls off the tongue, ignites curiosity, and begs investigation.

The Rise and Fall of Alcohol Prohibition
in Washington County, Arkansas

Pioneers who settled Washington County and other areas of the state in the early 1800s would have been shocked and highly annoyed with laws passed before the end of the century which regulated and ultimately prohibited the production and use of alcoholic drink. Personal freedoms taken for granted by men who forged the frontier slowly eroded as reform elements in society attempted to change the nation's drinking habits. Instead of men guiding their own 'manifest destiny,' those who considered themselves "God's defenders" presumed to know what was best for every man. Along with such moral regulations, however, came an onerous cost to the young nation as commonly accepted behavior became criminalized. Inevitably, the rule of morality would be replaced by the rule of outlaws.

Like the proverbial camel's nose under the tent, earliest efforts to regulate alcohol in Washington County were relatively benign and of an arguably reasonable nature. Local laws followed actions by the territorial legislature in 1802 which forbid the sale of "any spirituous, vinous, or other strong liquor" to Native Americans and a second action in 1820 requiring licenses for taverns and imposing a tax on distilleries in order to secure revenue for government operations.[15] Essentially unenforceable, the laws nevertheless made it possible for local authorities to single out particularly troublesome owners of dram shops and taverns for prosecution.

Washington County's position on the state's western boundary adjacent to the newly formed Indian Territory, caused its citizens

---

[15] Johnson p 7

to remain keenly interested in keeping strong drink from the hands of Natives. The threat of the unknown "Other," loosened by spirits and—arguably justly—incited to violence, drove such regulations. As a general rule, drink among responsible white men did not provoke fear or condemnation. Consumption of alcohol had been part of a long-standing cultural tradition that came to the New World along with the colonists.

With Arkansas statehood in 1836 came a more coherent public policy regarding alcohol. Among the first acts of the state legislature were regulations allowing municipalities and other local governmental entities to license taverns or even stop the sale of alcohol within their jurisdictions. But temperance held little attraction among a majority of Southerners whose culture included respect for those who could "hold their liquor" and even less appeal among freeholders who believed they had the right to do whatever they wanted on their own land including turning a modest portion of their grain crops into whiskey. Most alcohol manufacturing took place locally, some for personal use only but often by men who owned taverns or dram shops, and made use of nearby agriculture, turning a bulky commodity into a valuable and more easily transportable item.

As noted in the 1989 *History of Washington County*, "whiskey [was] a favorite and widely used medicine, a handy trade item, [and] the elixir of pioneer social intercourse."[16] So a more common-sense approach for local government was to regularly remind dram shop and tavern owners to renew their licenses, thereby augmenting operational funds for the government and appeasing abstainers with a modicum of regulation. Even this relatively mild hand of government chafed some, who followed the tradition of

---

[16] History of Washington County p 135

earlier colonists who—in the fine tradition of all things American—had rebelled against George Washington's first efforts to gain government revenue by taxing liquor. In the infamous 1791 Whiskey Rebellion, farmers raised the familiar cry of "no taxation without representation" and refused to pay. By 1794, the rebellion had gained strength and a body of five hundred armed rebels rode to protest at the western Pennsylvania home of the local tax agent. Their forces dissolved when Washington sent over 13,000 militia in response. The protesters resorted to illegal, moonlight distillery operations in order to avoid paying taxes on their drink. Thus began the venerated tradition of moonshine.

The term "dram shop" as it appears in laws of the time was often used interchangeably with "tavern," although the term originally referred only to establishments which sold liquor by the dram. One dram is technically a very small measurement equal to about one teaspoon. Informally, a dram could be any small amount of liquor. Such measurement of whiskey derived from Scotland, where the word "dram" was often prefaced by "wee," and which even now may refer to any modestly-sized drink of the good stuff, depending on the occasion and company. Similar terms would include drop, jigger, shot, sip, tot, nip, slug, or snort. "Dram shop" remains a legal term referring to establishments which dispense alcohol by the drink and which are subject to regulation by the state government. Taverns, on the other hand, were originally places where travelers could obtain lodging and food, as well as drink. Because they provided alcoholic drink, both types of establishments were required to obtain a license in early Washington County.

By the mid-19th century, increasingly targeted by the temperance movement, dram shop owners became legally liable for any untoward results of over-serving patrons, a concept that remains in force today.

Regulation of Alcohol in the 1830s

During the first decade of Washington County records, the following local men and/or partnerships obeyed the law and obtained license for a Dram House or Liquor sales:

> 1835
>
> A. & I. D. Parks, Cane Hill
>
> 1836
>
> James P. Hume
>
> McGarrah & Hubbard, Fayetteville
>
> James Moore, Cane Hill Township (Twp)
>
> Boice Walker
>
> Willis Wallace, Fayetteville
>
> Wilson & Brothers, Vineyard Twp
>
> 1837
>
> Samuel M. Cowdry, Vineyard Twp
>
> Henry Cureton

McGarrah & Hubbard, Fayetteville
Shannon & Harnage, Vineyard Twp
George Spencer, Cane Hill Twp
Willis Wallace, Fayetteville
Wilson & Brothers, Vineyard Twp

1838
James Barnes, Vineyard Twp
John Fitzgerald, Prairie Twp
Matthew Hubbard, Fayetteville
E. W. McClellan, Boonsboro
Moore & Allen, Cane Hill Twp
Willis Wallace, Fayetteville

1839
Calvin Cole, Illinois Twp
Charles Delaney, Vineyard Twp
Gillett & O'Bryant, Fayetteville
Matthew Hubbard, Fayetteville
Johnson & Kinnida
McRary & Donals, Illinois Twp
O'Bryant & Gillett, Illinois Twp
John Reagan, Illinois Twp
Safford & Pollard, Fayetteville
Sneed & Baltz, Fayetteville
Willis Wallace, Fayetteville

A tavern license was issued in 1837 to John Bostic of Fayetteville, who was likely not the only inn keeper of the county who served alcohol at this time. By 1839, more inn keepers had been brought into the fold:

James Byrnside, Fayetteville
John W. Onstott, Fayetteville
John M. Shuckley, Fayetteville

Wilson & Brother, Vineyard Twp

Many of the names listed above can be found in chronicles of early county life. Sons of Fayetteville's reputed first settler James McGarrah, both John McGarrah and his brother William sold liquor and also entered into business partnerships which were licensed in Fayetteville. According to one family historian, "William McGarrah opened a store at present site of the Hilton Hotel [southeast corner of East and Meadow, more recently The Chancellor]... April 11, 1836, Judge J. M. Hoge directed the court clerk to 'pen to William McGarrah and Mathew Hubbard a dram shop license' for a twelve month period to retail spirituous liquors in Fayetteville, upon sheriff's receipt of $20." In an 1860 interview, it was reported that "by the time a few people had settled around Fayetteville [John McGarrah] had entered into 'business' selling 'as good an artikel of them ar sperits as was ever fetch down the Massasippy.' For a long time he sold 'them ar.'"[17]

Purveyors of alcoholic drink in the county's other early settlements included Calvin Cole at Summers, located at the edge of Indian Territory and previously part of a land grant to the Cherokee. Calvin was the oldest son of John Cole who is said to have been the first landowner in that area. John served as postmaster (at Sylva) and after later moving to Texas, practiced medicine and pharmacy. Calvin's commercial enterprise was likely at Summers or possibly Cincinnati.[18]

South of Summers at Cane Hill, also near the state's western border, James Moore sold alcohol by 1836, was partner in the 1838 Moore & Allen license, and was probably related to R. T. Moore licensed also at Cane Hill in 1840. Also at Cane Hill, Evan White

---

[17] *History* p 1217
[18] *History* p 927-9

McClellan, son of illustrious Revolutionary War hero William McClellan, took over the Cane Hill properties of his father in 1842. Along with co-founding the state's first college there, the McClellans operated local steam mills, stores, and other thriving commercial enterprise.[19]

John Fitzgerald, who later operated a stagecoach stop on the north Washington County portion of the Butterfield Road, would have considered strong drink one of the necessities of his accommodation for those undertaking an arduous journey on the overland mail route between St. Louis and San Francisco. Likewise, James Byrnside's early log cabin Fayetteville inn, later called Byrnside Tavern, catered to weary travelers with hot food and warming drink.[20]

Arrests during the county's early years reveal something of the nature of men who moved into these new wilderness lands and also provide a view of the role of alcohol and its prohibition in the

---

[19] Ibid p 607
[20] Campbell p 5-6

crime rate. Washington County's first arrest, in 1829, was Hiram Johnson, for larceny. Details of his crime are not described in these early, handwritten records. But soon after, in 1830, Samuel Lowell was arrested for selling whiskey to Indians, while nine men were charged with assault and battery including several probably-related Williams kinsmen: Thomas, Frances (twice), Ambrose, and Samuel. Four counts of trading with Indians, against J. M. Graham, were dismissed.

In 1831, ten men were charged with assault and battery (including some of the Williams bunch, Frances and James), two for "gaming," one for horse stealing (later found not guilty), one for slander, and one with selling liquor to an Indian. Two men, Sebron Sneed and Reuben Reynolds, were charged both with gaming and assault and battery.

In 1832, five assault and battery arrests were made (including a woman named Sally Davidson), with one for murder, one for accessory to murder, two for gaming, three for "laboring on the Lord's Day," two for passing counterfeit money, one for selling spirituous liquor on the Sabbath, and two for selling liquor without a license. Three of the charges involved one man, Isaac Crow, likely for one incident involving the Sunday sale of liquor without a license.

Licensee Willis Wallace, son of early Fayetteville settler William Wallace, gained notoriety over an incident in 1839. According to a Wagnon family historian, John and Thomas Wagnon along with their brother-in-law John Curry "were engaged in a card game on Sunday morning in Fayetteville. Several citizens including a Willis Wallace attempted to put a stop to the game. A fight ensued. Wagnon escaped town with the money but Curry and several others were killed by this Wallace. Wallace was a known killer, killing even after this episode. He went to trial but was acquitted and lived his life out in Texas." (History p 1450) It is not recorded whether alcohol played a part in the incident.

Of the county's 2182 inhabitants in 1830, there was an average of 15 criminal indictments/court actions per year, or about .07% of the population.

The 1840s

As early as the American Revolution, a temperance movement had begun to take shape in a few states where farmers wanted to ban whiskey distilling. A national society had formed by 1826 which within the next twelve years claimed 8000 local chapters and over a million members. England, Australia, and New Zealand joined in the fervor, which at this point had mostly focused on distilled spirits without particular condemnation of wine or beer.

The national temperance movement gained strength from the religious fervor of the Second Great Awakening, an embrace of emotional rather than the more rational and deist approaches to religious faith. The need for a reduction of everyman's regular use of drink also sprang in part from the need for a sober workforce to man the machines of the increasingly industrialized economy. As the movement grew, the concept of "teetotalism" came into favor, and any form of alcohol was considered the Devil's work.

As noted in Ben Johnson's 2005 chronicle of alcohol regulation in Arkansas, *John Barleycorn Must Die,* Washington County's county seat Fayetteville hosted a well-established temperance movement by 1841, at which time the local chapter was humiliated by the discovery that its vice president had fled to Texas after embezzling over $20,000 through his job at the bank. (Johnson 12) Stirred to greater vigilance by this event, the society publically excoriated a member who confessed to drinking wine. In another "outing," the society issued a summons against such noteworthy local citizens

as Joseph J. Wood, John J. Stirman, and H. J. Sanderson for "the violation of their pledge to said Society." According to an account of the Fayetteville Temperance Society 1841-1844, published in the *Arkansas Historical Quarterly*, "Sanderson arose and publicly confessed that he frequently drank Ardent spirits and sometimes to excess." The Society approved a motion to report him as a person unworthy of membership.

Fayetteville's 1840s newspaper *The Witness* ("The Voice of the People in the Will of God") ran notices of the Society's meetings, which stated that "At said time and place all friends to the cause of temperance and all who would become members of the society are requested to attend." An article published February 16, 1841, noted: "At the adjournment of the Temperance Meeting held in this place on Monday evening last, we learn there was an accession of fifty new members. We have been informed by an officer of the society that it now numbers in all over one hundred and thirty persons, among whom were many who were heretofore conceived to be irreclaimable tipplers."

[At roughly this same time period, in adjacent Johnson County, Clarksville's society claimed 300 membership and in nearby

Sebastian County, Fort Smith counted 100. (Johnson 12)]

The article continued: "The general appearance of our town has quite altered. We see but little lounging in the groceries, or about grocery doors. [During this period, 'grocery' was a disparaging term which referred to taverns or other places which sold alcoholic drink.] Each man appears civil and well-disposed toward his neighbor, and instead of indulging in wrangling and rioting, engages in rational conversation or reading, and minds his own business. Our churches are generally well filled; and there is not so much *dodging in at grocery doors after service*, as formerly. Those few topers who are left, are even *said* to wear a shamed face when caught in the act of using 'the article.' We hope the time is not far distant when every citizen will use his influence to forward and establish upon a sure basis this commendable and praiseworthy association." [italics in original]

Among other items in these pages of *The Witness* was notice by the Fayetteville Academy, which listed its terms, trustees, and other operational details including: "III. No scholar shall frequent a grocery, either with a view of drinking himself, or being amused by those who may be intoxicated."

Such pious announcements notwithstanding, the newspaper publisher kept a steady eye on its business of making money. Its list of agents included at least one licensed dram shop owner, Mr. E. W. McClellan for Cane Hill. The paper also accepted advertisement for liquor from such regional concerns as Scott, White, and Co. of Van Buren, who routinely advertised "Groceries – Just received and for sale low for CASH, 20 sacks Havana and Rio Coffee, 20 boxes Sperm candles ... 20 kegs best Pickles ... 3 pipes best Cogniac Brandy, 10 bbls Molasses; 2 tierce Rice, 40 boxes best Havana Cigars ... 100 sacks Salt, 200 bbls Whiskey ... Lead and Powder, &c., &c." The paper also included a regular advertisement for "Entertainment" from John H. Newman of Ozark, who noted that "This subscriber takes this method of announcing to the public that he has again taken possession of the Tavern house formerly occupied by him in the Town of Ozark. Grateful for the liberal patronage heretofore received, he will spare no pains to accommodate those who may favor him with a call."

In general, the Arkansas laws regulating alcohol and the enforcement thereof did not reflect the intolerance of temperance activists. A united effort by state temperance chapters in 1842 to push through legislation prohibiting alcohol sales, or even substantially increasing licensing fees, failed.

The record of Washington County licenses issued in the 1840s for dram houses or liquor sales continued to include names of the county's upstanding citizens:

>1840
>B. Hoomenbarger, Fayetteville
>Matthew Hubbard, Fayetteville
>Jenks & Wilson, Vineyard Twp
>Bartley Johnson, Vineyard Twp
>Jesse Mayfield, Vineyard Twp
>John McGarrah, Fayetteville
>R. T. Moore, Boonsboro
>O'Bryant & Gillett, Fayetteville
>Elijah O'Bryant, Illinois Twp
>B. H. Smithson, Fayetteville
>Edward C. Sneed, Fayetteville
>Nathaniel Wafford, Vineyard Twp
>
>1841
>John Ballard, Hillsborough
>John Bostic, Vineyard Twp

Elkins & Davis, Evansville
Gillett & O'Bryant, Fayetteville
George Herndon, Fayetteville (married Cynthia McGarrah, daughter of John McGarrah)
Hubbard & Lynch, Fayetteville
McClellan & McClure, Boonsboro
Joseph Moore, Fayetteville Race Track*
Elijah O'Bryant, Illinois Twp
Pollard & Safford
N. & C. Wafford, Vineyard Twp
Leonard Wallace (Willis' youngest brother)

* Joseph Moore was the son of Samuel Moore, lieutenant in the War of 1812 and close friend of Andrew Jackson. The Moores settled near Fayetteville in 1836, where they farmed land now at the intersection of Highways 112 and I-49. The site included Joseph's horse racing track by the 1840s.[21]

1842
Alfred Chandler, Illinois Twp
Gillett & O'Bryant, Fayetteville
George Herndon, Fayetteville
Hubbard & Lynch, Fayetteville
McClellan & McClure, Boonsboro
Norman & Rowan, Vineyard Twp
John F. Safford, Fayetteville
B. H. Smithson, Fayetteville
William Vining, Hillsborough

1843
George Herndon, Fayetteville
Hubbard & Lynch, Fayetteville

---

[21] History p 952

McClellan & McClure, Boonsboro
William McGarrah, Fayetteville
Elijah O'Bryant, Illinois Twp

1844
Milton Breedlove, Fayetteville
Henry Hill, Fayetteville
Ezekiel Lane, Fayetteville
Devault Martin, Evansville
McClellan & McClure, Boonsboro
William McGarrah, Fayetteville
Granville B. Shannon, Evansville
Maurice Wright, Boonsboro

1845
Jacob Coats, Fayetteville
Tandy Kidd, Van Buren Road near Cane Hill
Ezekiel Lane, Fayetteville
Devault Martin, Evansville
William McGarrah, Fayetteville
Granville B. Shannon, Evansville
Maurice Wright, Boonsboro

1846
Jacob Coats, Fayetteville
John Grant, Fayetteville
Henry Hill, Fayetteville
Ezekiel Lane, Fayetteville
Devault Martin, Evansville
William McGarrah, Fayetteville
Granville B. Shannon, Evansville
B. H. Smithson, Fayetteville
T. C. Wilson, Boonsboro
Maurice Wright, Boonsboro

1847

George Herndon, Fayetteville
Tandy Kidd, Van Buren Road
Devault Martin, Evansville
William McGarrah, Fayetteville
Granville B. Shannon, Evansville
Charles Wafford, Vineyard Twp
F. C. Wilson, Boonsboro
N. B. Wilson, Fayetteville

1848

McCracken & Hood, Vineyard Twp
William McGarrah, Fayetteville
Granville B. Shannon, Evansville
Smith & Freyschlag, Vineyard Twp
William A. L. Throckmorton, Fayetteville
Charles Wafford, Vineyard Twp

1849

Devault Martin, Evansville
James McCracken, Vineyard Twp
William McGarrah, Fayetteville
Safford & Pollard, Prairie Twp
Granville B. Shannon, Evansville
William A. L. Throckmorton, Fayetteville
Henry Wilson, Boonsboro

Tavern licenses during this period were as follows:

1841

John W. Onstott, Fayetteville

1842

James Byrnside, Fayetteville
John W. Onstott, Fayetteville

1845
Tandy K. Kidd, Van Buren Road
William McGarrah, Fayetteville
John W. Onstott, Fayetteville

A review of the circuit court record in the period 1840-1842 finds 37 actions for assault and battery, five arrests for murder, two for rape, one for robbery, one for stabbing, one for shooting, two for shooting with intent to kill, one for challenge to a duel, and two for malicious mischief, eight for larceny, eight for "affray" (an act of suddenly disturbing someone), one for riot, with eight for gaming, two for keeping a gaming house and one for permitting gaming, nine for breaking the Sabbath, two for horse stealing and one for obstructing the public road.

Alcohol law violations were for retailing liquor without a license and another alcohol related indictment for keeping a tavern without a license against James Byrnside, which must have come as an unfriendly reminder to Mr. Byrnside that he had failed to annually tithe the local government even though he had obtained license in 1839. A charge against William Vining overlooked his one-time 1842 license to operate a dram shop, possibly triggered by his arrests for gaming and for permitting gaming.

Out of the 1840 population of 7148, an average of 31 arrests per year constituted .04% of the county's citizenry.

The 1850s

Conflicting national interests over the issue of slavery siphoned some of the energy out of temperance efforts during the 1850s. In some regions, teetotalers forced through laws banning dram shops, taverns, and other purveyors of drink. In Washington

County, business continued as before.

Dram shop and liquor licenses issued the first half of the decade were as follows:

1850
Thomas H. Boyce, Fayetteville
Thomas Jackson, Cincinnati
Devault Martin, Evansville
William McGarrah, Fayetteville
W. H. Rhea, Illinois Twp*
Granville B. Shannon, Evansville
William A. L. Throckmorton, Fayetteville
John W. Wilson, Boonsboro

*Son of the pioneer Rhea family of western Washington County, William reportedly opened a store in thriving Cincinnati in 1851. "The town had a certain attraction to outlaws who escaped justice by hiding in the Indian Nation, but who came to Cincinnati for supplies and to gamble at a hotel called the Cincinnati House. The gambling seems to have attracted a significant number of the get-rich-quick crowd, for one winter night in 1856 William was enticed into gambling. After playing all night he had won a pot worth thousands of dollars. It is said he decided not to gamble anymore and instead to go into the milling business. The big winnings from the Cincinnati House were invested in what was called the finest mill ever built west of the Mississippi." Local histories fail to mention what role whiskey may have played in William's success.[22]

1851
D. W. Denningberg, Evansville
Jefferson Eldridge, Evansville

---

[22] History of Washington County p 158-9

E. S. Liles, Fayetteville
Devault Martin, Evansville
William McGarrah, Fayetteville
Baxton Raper, Evansville
William H. Rhea, Cincinnati
Granville B. Shannon, Evansville
Thomas Taylor, Cincinnati
William A. L. Throckmorton, Fayetteville

1852
John M. Bell, Marrs Hill, Twp
William C. Harris
Legg & Bright, Vineyard Twp
E. S. Liles, Fayetteville
I. F. Marrs, Evansville
Devault Martin, Evansville
William McGarrah, Fayetteville
David A. Price, Cincinnati
Thomas Taylor, Cincinnati
William A. L. Throckmorton, Fayetteville
Charles Wafford, Vineyard Twp
John W. Wilson, Boonsboro

1853
James C. Hodges, Fayetteville
Kyrkendall & Barron, Mountain Twp
E. S. Liles, Fayetteville
Thomas R. Marquis, Cincinnati
Devault Martin, Evansville
William McGarrah, Fayetteville
Meredith Oxendine, Vineyard Twp
William A. L. Throckmorton, Fayetteville

1854
Liles & Thomas, Fayetteville

By 1850-1852, arrests for assault had decreased to 22, with two for affray, seven for larceny, and one each for bastardy, mayhem, maiming, assault with intent to inflict bodily injury, assault with a deadly thing, and accomplice to murder. There were up to seven arrests for murder (mostly Native American victims) and four for assault with intent to kill. Gaming resulted in twelve arrests.

Two licensed liquor retailers were arrested for selling spirits to a slave (William Throckmorton, William McGarrah). One person was arrested for selling liquor without a permit.

Three arrests of Throckmorton were two of the county's 22 arrests for assault as well as one of the gaming charges. His name also appears with an assault charge in the 1840-42 period. Yet William Throckmorton, son of esteemed Fayetteville physician and brother to an early Texas governor, seemed to have suffered no deleterious effects from his criminal behavior. He sat on a Washington County jury in 1843, served as a justice of the peace in 1850-51, performed marriages, and held the position of deputy sheriff in 1854 and possibly longer. While serving in the Mexican War (1847), William rode alongside the esteemed Colonel Archibald Yell. He later reported that he had been "by Yell's side when killed and that he deliberately charged the line of gleaming lances, rising in his stirrups and sabering right and left until unhorsed. ...William ever declared that he avenged the death of Yell by running the lancer through on the spot." (Campbell p 44)

Advertisements by local merchants during this period offered a wide range of alcoholic drink available to the public. In 1853, Liles & Thomas advertised "the best family supplies," confectionery, and "mackerel, Scotch herring, sardines, lobsters, and fresh fat oysters, hermetically sealed and prepared for immediate use," along with "Liquors: Cognac and American brandies, Bourbon and all the celebrated brands of cincinnati whiskies, Geneva, pure claret, sweet wine, port wine, Malga, Teneriffe, Madeira, and Champagne Wines! New Ark Cider, cherry bounce, brandy cherries, cordials, etc." (*South-West Independent* 1853)

Reflecting the increasing regulation and growing public hysteria about alcohol use under the incitement of temperance activists, the issuance of licenses in Washington County dropped off dramatically by the mid-1850s. In 1855, the Arkansas legislature passed a law allowing local townships to vote whether to allow alcohol sales within their boundaries. Fayetteville's newspaper the *South-West Independent* carried frequent comment on this state of affairs, the tenor of which insinuates the editor's low regard for such efforts, such as this February 10, 1855, piece:

> Bear it in mind, that the law now in force, in regard to retailing ardent spirits, requires the individual wishing to set up a dram shop to present to the county court a petition signed by *a majority of* the voters of the township in which the grocery is to be located, before he can obtain license to retail drams!

> Some of these petitions are already before the people, and it will soon be tested whether a majority of voters of Washington county are in favor of retail liquor shops or not. We believe, however, that there is, at present, only one licensed grocery in the county, and it may be that the hundred dollar tax will prevent the test from being applied to all but Prairie township; if so, the present law will affect only the people in and about Fayetteville. Practically, the passage of this law can affect Washington county but little. Still, for its moral effect, the public mind ought to be wide awake upon the subject, and act from principle.

How would it do to hold public meetings and have a little free discussion upon the subject? We make the suggestion and hope to see it acted upon; in this way both sides of the question may be freely and fairly presented to the public. We want the test to be a fair one."

February 17, 1855, a citizen's opinion voiced the opposing view:

To the Citizens of Prairie Township. By an act of our late Legislature, it devolves upon you, the independent voters of this Township, to say whether or not our county seat shall still be cursed with Licensed Dram Shops. The dram-seller is now forced to come to you personally and solicit your votes– to ask your signatures to his petition, for the privilege of retailing Ardent Spirits. He must seek many of you at your own homes, surrounded by your families – your wives and your children – and there, in that sacred retreat, ask you to aid him in erecting a Temple upon whose unholy shrine will be sacrificed the peace, happiness, and fondest and most cherished hopes of many a family–the sacred affection of homes–the health, wealth, credit, good name, moral feeling, integrity, and all good and noble aspirations of many in whose happiness and well-being, you, perhaps possess a deep and abiding interest.

It has been argued, and will still be urged to you, that if retail shops are proscribed, the evils of Intemperance will not be, in the least, diminished! ... [But] are you willing to see your names upon the public records as petitioners for a dram shop? Are you willing that in coming years, the bereaved and suffering widow, whose bitter despairing tears have bedewed the hopeless grave of a drunken husband, that the beggared neglected orphan shall come up to our courthouse and find your names recorded as those who aided in rearing the haunt of temptation and sin, where the husband and father fell?

Are you willing that the citizens of other portions of our county and State, and strangers from other lands, when they come to Fayetteville, and see the drunken miserable wretches wallowing in the filth and mire of the streets, or brawling before the doggery door, may be able to go and read your names...?

Who ever heard of a decent grog shop? True, one may be conducted with a kind of relative decency; for as crime admits of deeper and darker shades, so may a doggery sink still lower and lower in the disgusting scale of loathsomeness and depravity! Go to the most respectable dram shop in the land, and what sickening odors greet your nostrils! What coarse, brutal, obscene and blasphemous sounds penetrate your ears!...

[The author, signed "ANTI-GROCERY" continues for most of two columns.]

Meanwhile, clever profit-minded men set about providing the public with a more socially-acceptable alternative that still offered users a means to intoxication. Maine was among the first states to pass laws restricting liquor sales. And it was in Maine that David Hostetter went into business with his concoction of famous "bitters". With an estimated 39% alcohol content, the product rapidly gained widespread popularity. Based on a review of federal revenue stamps, one researcher calculated that between 1863 and 1883, Hostetter's generated about one million dollars per in retail sales. At the time of his death in 1888, Mr. Hostetter left an estate worth over $18 million.[23]

---

[23] Young

Fayetteville's newspaper ran wry observances on this state of affairs. For example, on June 16, 1855:

> 'Well, old fellow, what are you going to do, now the Maine Law is passed?'
>
> 'Do? Why, first rate, to be sure. I shall turn all my liquors together, spice them well, put them in half pint bottles, labeled Phenix Bitters, Schiedam Schnapps, or compound extract of Sarsaparilla, and in five years you will see me building a gingerbread palace on Fifth Avenue, with a private chapel and two parsons under regular salary. That's what I shall do!'

The same page included a piece entitled "Rattling" which stated, in part:

> Times are improving, decidedly. On Tuesday morning Dr. Stevenson filled our water-bucket with ice. Now how much more moral drinking had we than Danley with his vile rot-gut which he has been receiving for some time past, as presents, with fancy names, from some of the bars in his neighbors hard-by. There has been nothing in Little Rock for a year past but rot-gut; and Captain, your friends may send you around every day huge bumpers of palatable mixtures, but let them disguise them as they may, with ice, spices, and rare ingredients, you get nothing but rot-gut *still*...

> Whiskey drinking should assume a different phase in politics. Hitherto the question of prohibition has only been considered. Henceforth it should be regarded as a question of North and South. Whisky comes from Cincinnati, the great abolition hole of Ohio—the home of Harriet Beecher Stowe, the terminus of the underground railroad which freights our negroes to Canada. Now the abolitionists desiring, at all times and by all means, to injure the South, make their whisky as poisonous as possible... How can you drink Cincinnati whisky? If you must needs drink whisky, drink Bourbon...

And in an adjacent column:

> Danley and Dick are belaboring one another dreadfully about whisky. Now the whole cause of dispute is this: Each thinks the other's whisky better than his own. Both are deceived. If they will swap, Danley will find Dick's jug rot-gut, and Dick will find Danley's rot-gut.

In spite of the peppered public dialogue that took a rather long view of temperance arguments, subsequent issuance of licenses reflected the very restricted landscape for retail liquor establishments in Washington County. But although the more vocal constituency ruled the day, the government's encroaching disregard toward long-held drinking rights provoked more than one outcry, no doubt more so in private than in the public realm. One of Fayetteville's prominent merchants and licensed liquor retailer, J. C. Hodges, used his 1855 advertising space in the paper to voice his opinion, as presented in the adjacent column.

Well-paid advertising space ran in every issue for such conglomerations as Hostetter's Bitters and his competition, such as Comstock's Azor's Original Turkish Wine: "The great

FAYETTEVILLE FAMILY SUPPLY STORE

OWING to an enactment of the late Grand Solomonuc Legislature, and the will of the people, I have changed my step to suit the tune; and finding as the sale of liquors decreases that Family Supplies are more called for, I am determined to keep everything on hand from a goober pea to a sack of salt, from a lozenge to a hogshead of sugar; in short—provided they can be had at home or abroad—I shall keep all articles that can be called for in my line. I design to keep a full assortment of Confectionery and best Chewing Tobacco in town; the finest Cigars that Cuba can afford; a heavy supply of powder shot caps, and all sporting articles; all sorts of nuts and fruits, and condiments. My stock is full at present, and shall be enlarged as fast as purchases can be made. I shall keep on hand and sell in quantities prescribed by law, a choice selection of WINES and LIQUORS; and assure my friends whenever they have need of such for mechanical, scientific, medical, culinary and tonic purposes, they cannot do better than to call at the old stand. Attached to the other good things, the subscriber has not neglected the **SODA FOUNT**, which is now bubbling up nectar for the dry, the temperate, the way-farer and everybody else. Call in friends, and examine to your satisfaction. *Tempora mutantur et nios mutamur in illis.* Inasmuch as the above articles cost cash and we have paid it out, we would take it as a peculiar favor if all who are indebted to us would come and the red fork over.   J. C. HODGES,
W. side pub. sq. next to the Washington House.
Fayetteville, June 16, 1855.   40tf

remedy for general debility, weakness, loss of appetite... The WINE is the most pleasant and effectual remedy... It is so agreeable to the taste that any one asking it soon prefers it to any other wine..."[24]

A history of Comstock's various patent medicines including Azor's Turkish Wine finds that laudanum, a preparation of alcohol and opium, was on the short list of ingredients routinely used in their formulations.[25] Such "medicines" containing opium were considered miracle cures at the time, a period before the addictive properties of opium had been recognized.

Licenses issued in the rest of the decade were:

1855

James C. Hodges, Fayetteville

1856

Burrell Featherstone, Fayetteville

James C. Hodges, Fayetteville

1857

Walter Asher, Marrs Hill Twp

Stephen P. Ellis, Fayetteville

---

[24] South-West Independent June 16, 1855

[25] Shaw

James C. Hodges, Fayetteville

McRoy & Job, Fayetteville

1858

James Barnes, Fayetteville

James C. Hodges, Fayetteville

John M. Sharp, Liberty Hill

Thomas M. Williford, Fayetteville

1859

James C. Hodges, Fayetteville

John M. Sharp, Liberty Hill

1860

William R. Dye, Hog Eye

James Malicoat, Hog Eye

Only two licenses were issued for the operation of a tavern during the 1850s: William Adams in 1855, Fayetteville, and John W. Onstott in 1856, Fayetteville.

An average of 22 arrests per year for the 9970 inhabitants comprised .02 of the county's population in 1850.

The 1860s and War

With the approach of the War Between the States, public attention diverted from talk of temperance. In 1860-61, there were eleven arrests for alcohol offenses: three for selling spirits to a slave, three for retailing "ardent spirits" without a license, one for selling liquor in Illinois Township (Cincinnati) which by this time had voted itself dry, and four for selling liquor to an Indian.

Other "morals" arrests were eleven for breaking the Sabbath (playing cards), thirteen for gaming, two for cohabitation, and one for disturbing a religion congregation. Property offenses included three larceny indictments and one for receiving stolen goods. Nine persons were indicted for disturbing the peace in various incidents.

A total of 64 indictments for violence were leveled: three for murder, three for manslaughter, 46 for assault and battery, two for assault with intent to kill or do bodily harm, three for assault on an officer, six for assault with deadly weapon, and one for resisting an officer.

At the eve of the Civil War, an average 56 indictments of the county's 14,673 residents constituted nearly .04% of the population.

Fayetteville's new newspaper, *The Arkansian,* continued paid promotion of patent medicines such as Ayer's Cherry Pectoral, now known to have contained opium as a key ingredient, and Dr. Hoofland's German Bitters and his Balsamic Cordial. Also appearing on the newspaper pages were discreet notices of alcohol sales, such as the St. Louis enterprise under J. A. Monks which noted: "Parties may rely on getting a pure article of anything in my line. Choice old Bourbon whisky direct from Bourbon County Kentucky always on hand." Also advertising from St. Louis was a "Distillery Works" manufacturer: "Particular attention will be given to Copper and Brass Work for Distilleries, accommodating from one to two thousand bushels per day. Plans and models for the various kinds of Distilleries kept on hand for the accommodation of customers..." In the few extant editions of Fayetteville papers of the early 1860s, there seem to be no articles or editorials on the topic of temperance.[26]

Between 1862 and 1865, the Civil War utterly consumed the

---

[26] *Arkansian* Nov 9, 1860 through March 1861

nation's attention. Arkansas sided with the South, and Confederate leaders banned the manufacture of alcohol in order to conserve grain and other badly needed resources for the military. Most of the northern parts of the state fell to Federal control after 1862, and the region lapsed into guerilla warfare. Persons distilling and distributing whiskey received scant attention from would-be enforcers, but remained perpetually at risk of raids by those who wanted the product.

And the legal market for whiskey remained strong. Fayetteville's own David Walker, a community leader, legislator, and later Arkansas Supreme Court judge, made it known that he would pay "any price in or out of reason" for a supply of whiskey.[27]

The federal government had enacted an 1862 tax act to help pay for the war effort, including a tax on alcohol distilleries. Later these laws allowed federal agents widespread access to local "moonshiners." Following the war, social chaos allowed widespread freedoms for liquor manufacture and distribution among those who could obtain the necessary raw materials. Only the most conspicuous retailers would have felt compelled to seek out appropriate licensing.

Licenses issued for dram shops and taverns during this period were:

1865
Thomas Carter, Fayetteville

1866
James G. Angles, Fayetteville
Martin G. Bonham, Fayetteville
Thomas Carter, Fayetteville

---

[27] Johnson p 21

Henry Keiser, Fayetteville

1867
Henry Keiser, Fayetteville
Isaac Taylor, Fayetteville

1868
Thomas Carter, Fayetteville

The last of the tavern licenses were issued to Sarah Quarles, Fayetteville, July 13, 1867, and Susan H. Wing, Fayetteville, July 13, 1867.

On the heels of the war during the late 1860s, Fayetteville newspaper advertisements revealed a competitive saloon market and an accepting public attitude about drink. Taylor's Saloon & Billiard Room in 1868 advertised:

> Isaac Taylor having fitted up his new Marble bed Billiard Table, calls the attention of all lovers of the game, that they may pass pleasure's time, by calling at 1st door East of Baum & Bros. On Main street. Good order will be preserved. Cigars of the finest brands, constantly on hand. Also, Genuine Port Wine, Genuine Cogniac, Genuine Bourbon, Genuine French Brandy, Genuine Native Wine, Genuine Imported Wine.[28]

The Morning Star Saloon in the Pettigrew Building, south side of the Fayetteville Square, was an enterprise of Nolen & Carter:

> "Keeps constantly on hand the finest of Wine, Brandy, and Whiskey. Cigars, Oysters, Cheese and a general assortment of family groceries. They also have in connection with their saloon two excellent Billiard Tables, where lovers of this fascinating game can be accommodated at all times being day

---

[28] Fayetteville Weekly Democrat October 31, 1868

or night."

W. L. Nolen advertised prominently in 1869 as "Dealer in Wines, Brandy, Whiskies and all kinds of LIQUORS. I intend to make a specialty of selling only the very best quality of liquor that can be procured and customers can rely upon getting no other at my establishment. …Give me a call at the Saloon on the North side of Main street, third door from the square, Carter's old stand."

Kaiser's Saloon advertised "Bourbon, Rye and Corn Whiskey, Cogniac Brandy, Ale, Porter, Claret, Port Wine, Sparkling Catawba, Champagne, Sherry and Rum. Also a choice selection of Cigars, Tobacco, Oysters, Sardines &c., in fact everything usually kept in a first class saloon."

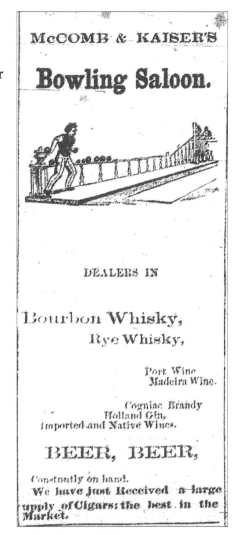

Kaiser joined with McComb for a separate enterprise, surely one of the more unique variations of the saloon business, a bowling saloon as shown in this 1868 ad (previous page).

Missing from the county's license registry were A. J. and S. J. Blackwell, of Blackwell & Bro., whose advertisements named their location at the "Northwest corner of the Public Square at the sign of the Big Barrel." They promoted themselves as "Wholesale and Retail Dealers in Foreign and Domestic LIQUORS, Wines, Brandies, Whiskies. 50 Barrels Whiskey on Hand. A choice lot of Fine Whiskies from E. Simpson & Co., New York."

The same page of the *Fayetteville Weekly Democrat* (July 1869) shows that druggists also advertised alcohol, which—in reaction to the temporarily-weakened temperance movement—was increasingly promoted as "medicinal." Dr. P. M. Cox listed "Fresh Drugs, Pure Drugs" along with "Fine Bourbon, Rye and Magnolia Whiskey, Fine French Brandies, Wines of various brands, Tonic Bitters, etc."

As the nation slowly regained its footing, the lingering effects of the temperance movement led to this new framing of alcohol as a medical tonic. And indeed, during the War, as medical supplies ran low especially in the South, field doctors were often forced to resort to the use of alcohol as an anesthetic for such procedures as amputation. Alcohol's ability to numb the emotions also served those well who had suffered loss of loved ones, homes, and dreams.

The 1870s

After the war, Washington County like the rest of Confederate Arkansas gained population from Northern states who sought economic opportunity in war-ravaged communities. Land was cheap and local power structures had been destroyed. Especially the northern counties saw an influx of entrepreneurs, including those interested in the production of strong drink, although not necessarily limited to distilled or malted spirits.

Philip and Kate Kessler established what may have been the state's first commercial winery when they came to Washington County in 1866 from Springfield, Missouri. According to an account of the family's enterprise in the February 1984 *Flashback*, Philip Kessler arrived with enough wealth to purchase prime land (now referred to as Kessler Mountain, southwest of the Cato Springs Road and I-49 intersection) where he immediately established a vineyard and winery.

Between 1869 and 1873, notices in local papers advertised a "full supply of native grape wines [and] celebrated Champaign Cider. The trade supplied for sale at Dorman's Bakery." Kessler's "Wine Halle" opened on West Center Street and included billiards.

Grand jury indictments in 1869-71, aside from numerous actions for debt, contempt, and trespass, were: nine for larceny, ten for grand larceny, three for burglary, one for fraud, one for robbery, sixteen for assault, two for assault with intent to harm/kill, four for murder, one for disturbing church, eight for breaking Sabbath, and 34 for gaming. The mood of the times evidently did not countenance legal action for mere use of intoxicating drink; there was only one alcohol related arrest, for "tipling."

Overall, an average annual 30 indictments comprised less than .02% of the county's 17,266 population in 1870, a remarkable fact considering the shredded social fabric of those times. The data may speak more about the lack of law enforcement and/or a nonfunctioning criminal justice system than any absence of criminal behavior.

General lawlessness following the Civil War caused communities to become increasingly intolerant of boisterous behavior. A population of distraught people shared the belief that alcohol intoxication was the primary cause of lawlessness. The resurgence of temperance societies led by charismatic speakers spread throughout the state. John Hallum, who served four terms during these decades as president of the State Prohibition Alliance of Arkansas, was later credited as pivotal in the Alliance's success in "the pioneer work that later brought prohibition to Arkansas."[29]

Such activist organizations and their efforts led to the development of licensing laws meant to restrict the availability of alcoholic beverages. In 1871 the state legislature passed laws allowed localities to forbid the sale of liquor within three miles of a college, which Fayetteville and Cane Hill soon enacted. The so-called local option law of 1879 became the instrument most useful in drying up liquor sales. It "required voters within a township or incorporated town to vote every two years on whether or not to permit the granting of licenses to sell alcohol in quantities of less than five gallons. If the license option failed to gain a majority, then saloons were out of business for at least two years." Most often, once voted dry, the jurisdiction never managed to go back to being wet.[30]

In reality, such changes did not take effect immediately. For

---

[29] Arkansas Historical Quarterly V 10 p 263
[30] Johnson 42

example, early 1870s advertisement of liquor stock available from Fayetteville merchants did not necessarily correspond with listed licensees. In advertisements running through the February 1870 editions of the *Fayetteville Weekly Democrat,* Isaac Taylor announced his "New Saloon," informing the public that he had "opened an entire new stock of Liquors at Taylor's old stand on Main Street, and will keep at all times the very best Brandies, Wines, Whiskies, Cigars and everything usually kept in a First Class Saloon." Blackwell continued to advertise their liquor goods, as did the pharmacist Cox.

By 1872, a new pharmacist J. C. Pendleton (successor to Peacock & Pendleton) promoted "Strictly Pure Wines and Liquors for Medical Purposes" along with his "chemicals, oils, patent medicine" and noted in fine print: "We are exclusive agent for the State of Arkansas for one of the best Distilleries of Kentucky, for their pure Bourbon Whisky, which we guarantee to be perfectly pure."

Punch cartoon 1874 showing gentlemen enjoying a social drink. The dress and glass size added humor to this social commentary.

1870s licenses for dram shops and liquor sales were:

1873
Reuben Carter, Fayetteville
Thomas Carter, Fayetteville
W. J. Gilliland, Fayetteville
John Reed, Hog Eye
Ewing G. Suttle, Fayetteville

1874
Reuben Carter, Fayetteville
John Reed, Billingsley

1875
A. E. Carney, Billingsley
William Smith, Spring Valley

1877
Alonzo Sawyer

The drop off in permits did not signal the end of interest in intoxicating drink. As noted in their article on Prohibition, the Encyclopedia of Arkansas states:

> In the post-war era, farmers found they could earn far greater profits by producing alcohol than by growing corn or other agricultural products. The spread of moonshine stills and the illegal trade in alcohol spurred response from Arkansas law enforcement. Throughout the 1870s, in what became known as the 'moonshine wars,' federal revenue agents (who assailed moonshine as a violation of the law because it was being sold without paying the requisite liquor tax) fanned out across the hilly terrain of northern Arkansas in search of illegal stills. Raids against moonshiners (also known as 'wildcatters') were common, and stories of violent shootouts were vividly recounted in local newspapers. Local officials often sided with

wildcatters in opposition to federal authorities, and jury nullification—in which accused wildcatters were given extremely light sentences or acquitted—was commonplace."[31]

Operating under the "Office of the Commissioner of Internal Revenue," reviled deputy commissioners, or "revenuers," ventured into the countryside searching out renegade distilleries. This stoked the ire of independent backwoodsmen in Arkansas, especially Confederate sympathizers who not only inherited a cultural appreciation of drink but who also despised the federal government. They became ingenious at hiding their stills and brazen in ambushing revenuers. During these years, the old Kessler wine cellars served as an ideal secret location for a productive distillation operation. For every license issued for legal alcohol sales in Fayetteville, there were no doubt a multitude of 'shine operations both within the city and out in the county, evidence for which is obvious in the continuing arrests for alcohol offenses.

The 1880s

1881 was a landmark year in Washington County for the issuance of dram shop and liquor sales licenses, with 13 permits granted–the greatest number of any year. The swell in numbers likely reflect efforts by local government to gain more control over alcohol distribution rather than any sudden desire on the part of the licensees to obey the law.

Paying their permit fees that year were:

>John H. Cato, Farmington
>Phillip Corrigan, Fayetteville
>Caleb Cox, Summit Home

---

[31] https://encyclopediaofarkansas.net/entries/prohibition-3002/

C. S. Gray, Fayetteville (physician)
J. W. Harman, Oxford's Bend
J. N. Lyles, Fayetteville
E. P. Neal, Crawford Twp
B. H. Payne, Eidson's Springs
W. H. Pitts, Fayetteville (two indictments)
Frederick Schmitzer, Crawford Twp
C. M. Sparkman, Crawford Twp
Whitlow & Lake (pharmacy), Fayetteville
T. H. Woolem, Summit Home

In 1882, '85, and '86, John H. Cato, Farmington, received the only license issued in Washington County. An amusing story is connected to Cato and his alcohol production. In 1876, he purchased a successful Farmington grist mill from Abe Allen, who was cousin to Farmington's founding father William Engles. Cato immediately built a whiskey distillery next to the mill, incurring the wrath of Engles who, according to *The History of Washington County,* was an "arch enemy of strong drink" and who had begun a campaign to have it outlawed in the area. Mr. Engles became outraged at this use of his former property, but could do nothing to stop it except lobby for stricter laws. Records fail to note whether Abe Allen had acted in full knowledge of Mr. Cato's plans, but some observers surmised that he did.

And stricter laws did have their effect in providing the criminal justice system greater power over persons involved in the alcohol trade. A review of the 1881-82 indictment record of the county reflects enforcement of such laws regulating alcohol sales. There were eleven indictments for providing liquor to a minor. There were eighteen counts of selling liquor within three miles of a college, four persons indicted with a total of fourteen counts for keeping a "dram shop and drinking saloon for the sale of malt liquors without a license," and four arrests for selling "ardent and fermented liquor without a license."

J. Harmon, licensed in 1881, was indicted that year for selling liquor to a minor. J. N. Lyles, also licensed, received two indictments for selling liquor within three miles of the University, four indictments for "keeping a dram shop and drinking saloon for the sale of malt liquor without a license," one count of selling a half gallon of ardent and fermented liquor, and two counts of selling malt liquor on the day of an election. [J. N. Lyles was the son of E. S. Liles, who had been licensed personally and as Liles and Thomas during the 1850s for dram shop operations in Fayetteville. J. N. clearly hoped to carry on the family business.]

James "J. H." Barnes, a 20-year-old Prairie Grove resident, received four indictments for keeping an unlicensed dram house/saloon, two counts of selling within three miles of Cane Hill college, one count each for selling one quart of liquor, for selling "intoxicating liquors commonly called tonics and bitters," and for selling to a minor.

Non-alcohol morals indictments in 1881-82 were eight for disturbing a religious congregation, 23 for breaking the Sabbath, two for cohabitation, 20 for gaming (involving $5 pots on "Pocre" or "Seven-up"), and one for "buggery upon a certain bitch and female dog." Property offenses included nine for failure to work/maintain the public road, one for killing fish by using an explosive in the Illinois River, two for financial fraud, two for larceny, and five for grand larceny.

Violence resulted in nine indictments for assault and battery, two for arson, four for attempting to "rescue" a prisoner, one for robbery, six for assault with deadly weapon, five for assault with intent to kill/do bodily harm, two for assault with intent to rape, and one for murder.

Offenses categorized as disturbing the peace totaled 27. The greatest number of charges were 52 for "wearing a weapon," a result of new laws attempting to separate men from ready use of arms. We have not included charges for this offense in our overall tallies or percentages.

An average of 90 indictments per year constituted nearly .04% of the county's 1880 23,844 population.

By 1888, there were seventy-five local temperance unions in Arkansas and a call for legislators to require schools to teach abstinence. The Hillhouse Act, passed by the legislature in 1899, put such material in classrooms. (Johnson 40) Sensitive to the public mood, Fayetteville merchants published notice of their wares whether licensed or not, although the text of such ads made it clear that the sale of alcohol for recreational consumption no longer occurred.

J. M. Whitworth, proprietor of the Iron Clad Drug Store advertised in the *Fayetteville Democrat* "Best of Wines and Liquors when used for Sacramental or Medicinal purposes. OTHERWISE NONE."

Whitlow & Lake, who were licensed in 1881, ran an ad series that year promoting their "New Drug Store" on the north side of the Square due west of McIlroy's Bank.

W. H. Whitlow dominated local drug store commerce, serving as a pharmacist and wholesaler. This did not, however, protect him from the law. George T. Lake and W. H. Whitlow received an

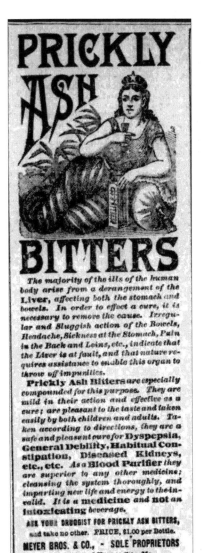

Appearing often throughout the 1880s in Fayetteville Weekly Democrat.

1883 indictment for selling within three miles of the city's new university.

By the end of 1882, no ads are found announcing where interested shoppers might buy whisky, even as medicine. However, patent medicine was conspicuously advertised on Fayetteville newspaper pages, and a multitude of drug store notices mention that "all drugs and medicines" are constantly in stock. Hostetter's Bitters were advertised in every edition.

One contemporary court review of such products, wherein prosecutors for several states brought suit, cited analysis specifically of Dr. B. F. Sherman's Prickly Ash Bitters to note that "one gill [four ounces, or one-half cup]...will produce intoxication." Observers wryly noted that by this time a substantial percentage of the male population had become afflicted with ailments requiring a doctor's prescription for medicinal spirits.[32]

With the local papers awash in promotions for drug stores and

---

[32] Johnson 43

patent medicines, the Washington County Grand Jury's Fall 1889 term produced indictments against fourteen men for selling liquor without a license, the greatest number of indictments being shared by Boyd and Bird Collier (seven).

The social impact of these proliferating temperance efforts is illustrated in the case of George Quick. As the moralist drums beat ever more loudly, this hapless young man received three indictments for "selling alcoholic ardent and vinous liquors and intoxicating spirits" without a license. His story has been fleshed from newspaper and court records.

On January 24, 1890, the *Fayetteville Democrat* (weekly) reported his arrest: "George Quick was arrested Saturday on the charge of selling whiskey, presented by the last grand jury. On default of bail, he was committed to jail." At the April 1890 session of the circuit court, George's bond hearing was first on the docket. His father James Quick posted his $250 bond.

State witnesses T. W. Thurman and W. E. Long failed to appear for the trial, as did William Horton, Jake Harmon, and Thomas Bynum for the defendant. These delays caused the case to be postponed to the Fall 1890 session, at which time the court required the witnesses to post a $200 bond each to ensure they would appear at future court dates. George's father maintained his cash bond for his son.

But at the Fall 1890 term, two key witnesses for George remained elusive. It was reported to the court that witness Bynum was in Monett, Missouri, but not "absent by the consent, connivance, or contrivance of the Defendant," according to Walker and Walker, legal counsel for George. By the same argument, George's other key defense witness Harmon was inconveniently in Greenwood

Arkansas, but was expected to be "here by next court."

George's attorneys entered a plea not guilty, and the court noted Mr. Quick's statement that "Bob Lee" was the one who sold the liquor. A motion was made for a change of venue, remarking that "the minds of the inhabitants of the county of Washington are so prejudiced against him that he cannot obtain a fair and impartial trial in said county." Testifying for the change request was the one available defense witness, Will Horton, who agreed that George couldn't get a fair hearing in Washington County.

The court granted a change of venue to Benton County. Benton County records show a court hearing in February 1891 but no disposition of the case was documented. Family records reveal that George died a month later on March 22, 1891, age 22. No place or cause of death is noted.

What role did George's arrest and prosecution play in his death? While there is no evidence that the arrest and prosecution led to his death, his legal woes would have exacerbated any other problems he may have been experiencing and added to the family's trauma. This case highlights the failure of prohibition laws to address root causes of a person's addiction and/or other dysfunctional behavior.

The 1890s

During the period of George's prosecution, Washington County's 1890-91 grand jury indictments included 45 charges of selling "alcoholic, malt, ardent, vinous, and intoxicating spirits" without a license and one charge of selling to a minor. Previously licensed J. H. Cato received three indictments in this period and J. Lyles received six.

Other morals complaints were four for illegal cohabitation, 22 for disturbing a religious congregation, eleven for breaking Sabbath (one instance of selling a suit of clothes, the rest for playing cards), and one for seduction, a crime wherein a man promised marriage, enjoyed certain affections from the woman, and then did not marry her.

Disturbing the peace produced 24 indictments with an additional fifteen for wearing weapons. Property offenses included three offenses for road work, three for fraud, one burglary, five larceny, eleven grand larceny, and one cruelty to animal. Violent acts resulted in four indictments for murder, two for manslaughter, two for robbery, 16 for assault and battery, five for assault with intent to kill, and five one for assault with deadly weapon.

An annual average of 82 charges involved slightly less than .03% of the county's 1890 population of 32,024.

By the end of the century, the state's Prohibition Party ran candidates for state and federal office. Temperance extremist Carrie Nation—later residing in nearby Eureka Springs—had begun her violent hatchet attacks on liquor supplies in Kansas saloons. Washington County's grand jury in 1899-1900 found 118 outrages worthy of their censure.

Alcohol offenses resulted in nineteen charges: six for giving away alcohol within three miles of a college, one for providing to a minor, and the rest for selling without a license, including a count against J. H. Cato.

Other morals charges were breaking Sabbath (3), disturbing church services (5), betting (3), cohabitation (2), and carnal knowledge of a child under 16 (1). Disturbing the peace resulted in 42 indictments, with another nine for weapons.

Property offenses included three for malicious mischief, three for fraud, one for burglary, six for larceny, and ten for grand larceny. Violence resulted in ten indictments for assault and battery, one for robbery, two for assault with intent to harm/kill, four for assault with deadly weapon, one for assault with intent to rape, one for manslaughter, and one for murder.

An average of 59 offenses per year comprised slightly less than .02% of the county's 34,000 population in 1900.

A New Century

In 1906, when 54 of Arkansas' 76 counties voted dry, the long effort toward prohibition began its final rise to glory. Saloons were outlawed, alcohol sales severely restricted, and persons desiring drink were forced to seek black market sources. Politicians who might support a person's right to drink ran for cover as temperance societies dominated the political landscape. Whatever voices called for reason or a man's right to choose had been effectively silenced.

In 1910-11, offenses in Washington County against the peace and dignity of the state included 99 alcohol related charges: a staggering 80 indictments for public intoxication, nine for providing liquor to a minor, one for procuring liquor for another in a prohibited district, three for selling within three miles of a college, and six for selling liquor without a license.

Other morals indictments were gaming (33), disturbing church services (21), and a variety of miscellaneous charges including giving medicine to induce an abortion, profanity, and seduction (7). Twenty one were charged with disturbing the peace and seven for wearing weapons. Eight persons were charged for malicious mischief, with other property crimes including two for fraud, one for larceny and two for grand larceny.

Violence occurred in ten assault and battery offenses, one assault with intent to inflict bodily harm, one with intent to rape, two as accessory to murder.

By 1910, an average of 109 indictments comprised just over .03% of the county's 33,889 population.

As prohibitionists gained strength, state law by 1915 reflected the anti-alcohol fervor. That year an Arkansas bill criminalized all production or sale of alcohol even as medicine, preceding national prohibition by four years. In 1917, state legislators enacted a further measure prohibiting any shipment of liquor into the state, removing local option in city or county and making Arkansas one of the first "bone dry" states. National prohibition, a constitutional amendment called the Volstead Act, went into effect October 28, 1919.

The effect of these laws rippled through the criminal justice system at all levels of local, state, and national government. In 1920, a total of 160 indictments/cases involved just over .04% of Washington County's population of 35,468.

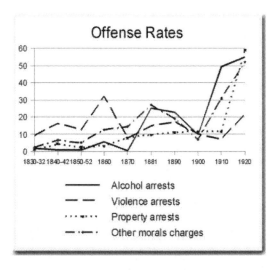

There were 18 charges related to alcohol: one for providing to a minor, four for selling without a license, two for transporting, one for public drunk and ten for manufacturing alcohol. The greater number of alcohol related arrests occurred in the new municipal jurisdictions, estimated to be over one hundred. Local jails and courtrooms strained to meet this new demand.

Other morals charges were 23 indictments for selling cigarettes, three for pandering, three for carnal abuse, one for cohabitation, two for breaking Sabbath, four for disturbing church, and sixteen for gaming. Property offenses included malicious mischief (7), road (1), burglary (7), larceny (1), grand larceny (33), and forgery or other fraud (10). Disturbing the peace charges were leveled against nine persons and another five were indicted for wearing weapons. Violence was involved in two arson offenses, three robberies, two assault with intent to rape, six assault and battery, and seven assault with intent to harm/kill, and two murder.
As shown on the adjacent chart, for Washington County, Arkansas, the move toward alcohol prohibition resulted in an increase in every type of crime, no doubt the opposite of the moralists' expectations.

In an effort to understand the personal and community effects of these changes, we examined the stories of five persons indicted in

1920, all members of the Ritchie family. According to public records, in September 1918, Christopher C. Ritchie, oldest son of Elias and Mary Ann "Polly" Ritchie of Delaney, had purchased over 500 acres in Hazel Valley near the headwaters of the Middle Fork of the White River. While newcomers to Washington County, Ritchie family members had been in the same general area on the Madison County side of the line for decades.

The Ritchie family originally had settled in northwest Arkansas shortly after the Civil War. Hiram and his wife Euphemy migrated from Kentucky and took up farming in the rich bottom lands of Madison County. Several children were born to this union, including Elias, who married a woman named Polly and established a homestead in the area now known as Delaney and Crosses in Madison County's Valley Township. Their son Christopher was born in 1873, and another five children would be born to Elias and Polly by 1886.

In January 1920 when the census enumerator came to Christopher's household near Osburn, Reed Township, Washington County, Christopher (45, farmer) and his wife Sarah Evoline (42) had a household including the following children: Lee 18 (teamster), Alton 16 (teamster), Bulah 14, Dorthy 12, James C. 10, Eli 8, and Thelma 3 months. Next door was the household of their oldest son Garland Ritchie (24, farmer) and his new wife Birdie Jewell, who was expecting their first child. Christopher had paid nearly $2000 for this rich bottomland along both sides of the Middle Fork of the White River, which was good farming land in an otherwise rugged and mountainous part of the county.

Indictments issued in 1920 accused Garland Ritchie and his brothers Lee and Alton, as well as their uncle Hiram Ely Ritchie (age 34 in 1920), of manufacturing alcohol in March of that year. Another indictment was issued for Christopher Ritchie, who was accused of disturbing the peace on April 22, 1920, and in particular disturbing the family of John Osburn, by running his horse on the public highway and using profane, obscene, violent, insulting language, and by making loud and unusual noise.

John Osburn was listed as one of the witnesses against the Ritchie boys and Christopher's behavior on April 22 occurred when the family became aware of Osburn's role in the charges against them. As part of the family for whom the settlement of "Osburn" was named, John evidently considered it his responsibility to report illegal liquor production in an operation near his family lands. The nature of the laws and hysteria surrounding enforcement of prohibition often pitted neighbors against each other in this manner and predated the modern terms "snitch" and "narc" to label those who "ratted out" people to law enforcement.

Christopher posted bond for himself in a $250 lien against his property, and also posted $750 bond each for Lee and Alton. On May 5, 1921, the circuit court under Judge W. A. Dickson heard the cases for Garland and Hiram, both of whom had remained in custody of Sheriff H. E. Jackson pending a hearing. Both pled guilty "of manufacturing liquor and places himself at the mercy of the court and the court being well advised in the premises doth fix said defendants punishment at imprisonment for one year in the Arkansas state penitentiary, whereupon the defendant in person in open court waives the time required by law for sentence and asks that he be sentenced now...to be safely and speedily transported to the penitentiary house, or state convict farm or camps of the state of Arkansas, and there confined at hard labor for the period of one year from this date..."

Shortly after this sentencing, deeds showing Christopher's transfer of land title to his wife Sarah were registered with the county. The bulk of the lands, an accumulation of roughly 423 acres, was deeded to Sarah in a document dated December 20, 1918, but not filed until May 23, 1921. An additional 108 acres were deeded to her May 13, 1921. This placed all the Christopher Ritchie lands into her name and raises the question of whether Christopher's original deed to her in 1918 had anticipated adverse results of moonshine production which he planned or had engaged in there.

Records from the Arkansas State Penitentiary state that Hiram Ritchie, Christopher's brother, was 35 years old, 132 pounds, five feet seven and one-half inches tall, with a fair complexion, brown hair and blue eyes. He reported a first grade education, employment as laborer, and his adherence to the "Holiness" faith. The Descriptive Register listed "one upper gold tooth, many small scars on head, 4 small scars left forearm."

Garland Ritchie, age 24, was 147 pounds, and five feet seven inches tall with a ruddy complexion, black hair, and brown eyes. He reported an eighth grade education, employment as farmer, and no religion. Marks included "quick [fresh] scar right side chest, scar left forefinger, two small scars on abdomen." Both men stated they were born at Crosses, Arkansas, and resided at Osburn. They were admitted to the state prison on May 15, 1921 and paroled on September 12 of that year, each serving four months of their year sentences.

In the October 1921 term of the circuit court, Christopher was fined $5 for his offense of disturbing the peace and both Lee and Alton were discharged from their indictments for liquor manufacturing in a *noll prosequi* action by prosecutor J. W. Nance.

The 1930 census shows that the extended Ritchie family had moved just across the Oklahoma line to Adair County.

Christopher and Sarah's household was one door away from Garland and Birdie at the county seat, Stillwell. Family records show that the birth of Garland's first child occurred in Oklahoma in 1920, suggesting that at least Birdie moved soon after the indictment.

Two additional children were born to Garland and Birdie in Oklahoma, in 1922 and 1929. Christopher lived until 1944, Sarah until 1946. Garland died in 1985 at Stillwell, and Alton in 1983 at Tahlequah. Lee remained in the family household at age 29, as shown in the 1930 census, along with Dora 24 and two young children listed as Christopher's grandchildren. These were likely Lee's family. He died in 1934 at the age of 33.

Christopher's brother Hiram (youngest child of Hiram and Euphemy) noted on his World War I draft registration that he was of Crosses, age 29, and a laborer at the Amos Martin Handle Company at Crosses. A month earlier he had joined the state guard, but noted on the registration form that he had "volunteered twice and been rejected." Genealogical records state that he served as a private in the U. S. Army during World War I, never married, remained in Delaney all his life, died after an extended illness in 1960 in Fayetteville, and was buried at the Walnut Grove Cemetery in Madison County.

Various details of the Ritchie family's activities suggest possible alcoholism. At first glance, the moralist might say the law protected them from themselves. But in fact, the law only added to whatever burden the family may have suffered from habitual or excessive use of intoxicating spirits, draining the family coffers of financial resources, uprooting them from a productive farm, and shaming them with the censure of neighbors and the government. In retrospect, little constructive result of such coercion can be found.

The Rise in Crime

The Ritchie family's imbroglio was only one of many such cases in the county, state, and nation to play out during that time. For the next fourteen years, unregulated alcohol production and sales spawned violence and lawlessness ultimately leading to the formation of powerful crime syndicates. Efforts at home production led to infamous bathtub gin and other poisonous brew. In an all-out effort to stop citizens from consuming illegal alcohol, the federal government intentionally contaminated industrial alcohol with deadly methanol, leading to the death of an estimated ten thousand Americans. Reminiscent of this mindset was the effort to stamp out Mexican marijuana crops in the 1970s and early 1980s by the use of herbicides like paraquat now known to cause Parkinson's disease.

Meanwhile, members of Congress and others in powerful positions continued to obtain alcohol and enjoy the pleasures of drink. Champagne and fine wine flowed freely in Washington D.C.'s private gatherings of politicians and lobbyists, courtesy of the French embassy. While enjoying their relative freedom from prohibition's restrictions, legislators created tax-supported agencies such as the Federal Bureau of Investigation.to better enforce those same laws against the taxpaying citizenry.

Steadily increasing allotment of tax dollars to support law enforcement efforts by local, state and federal agencies did little to staunch the rise of collateral damage to families and communities nationwide. Underground "speakeasies" and networks of bootleggers and rum runners gained public favor under widespread disrespect for prohibition laws. Criminal syndicates gained vast wealth by supplying forbidden drink to eager consumers and armed themselves with state of the art automatic weapons which they didn't hesitate to use in administering "street justice." Their wealth led to corruption of local governments, courts, and police forces by supplying campaign funds, cash gifts, and/or supplies of illegal whiskey to be sold or consumed.

What had been a man's private choice to consume alcoholic drink had now become a weapon against the very fabric of the nation, ironically the same language used by prohibitionists. In the name of morality, prohibition had led to an even greater abyss of immorality. Without the ability to see into every household, enforcement became a selective coercion against targeted individuals least able to defend themselves such as the poor and minorities.

Nationally, statistics of the period reveal the disastrous results of prohibition. According to later studies commissioned by President Nixon and compiled from government records:

> The early experience of the Prohibition era gave the government a taste of what was to come. In the three months before the 18th Amendment became effective, liquor worth half a million dollars was stolen from Government warehouses. By midsummer of 1920, federal courts in Chicago were overwhelmed with some 600 pending liquor violation trials. Within three years, 30 prohibition agents were killed in service.
>
> Other statistics demonstrated the increasing volume of the bootleg trade. In 1921, 95,933 illicit distilleries, stills, still works and fermenters were seized. In 1925, the total jumped

to 172,537 and up to 282,122 in 1930. In connection with these seizures, 34,175 persons were arrested in 1921; by 1925, the number had risen to 62,747 and to a high in 1928 of 75,307. Concurrently, convictions for liquor offenses in federal courts rose from 35,000 in 1923 to 61,383 in 1932.

Ironically, by the time the nation regained its senses and ended prohibition, enforcement of the law had declined dramatically. Arrests by federal marshals sat unprosecuted, stills and other manufacturing apparatus disappeared from evidence rooms, and the public mood had fully soured. Franklin D. Roosevelt won the Democratic nomination and subsequently the November 1932 vote for president on a platform that included repeal of prohibition.

On December 5, 1933, the nation's failed experiment in alcohol prohibition officially ended. Arkansas became fully "wet" for low content beer and wine until 1935, when a new state law allowed counties to vote themselves dry. It had been roughly 100 years along an expensive and destructive path from the time when Washington County's first settlers convivially shared homemade whiskey in the region's homes, dram shops, and taverns.

Sources cited in this article

Washington County Archives Indictments records and Miscellaneous Licenses records.

Arkansas Historical Quarterly, Arkansas Historical Society. Vol. 3 p 164-191 "Temperance" The Constitution and Proceeding of Fayetteville Temperance Society 1841-1844

Campbell, William S. *One Hundred Years of Fayetteville 1828-1928*, Washington County Historical Society, Fayetteville, Arkansas.

Johnson, Ben III. *John Barleycorn Must Die: The War Against Drink in Arkansas*. Fayetteville: University of Arkansas Press, 2005.

History of Washington County, Arkansas. Shiloh Museum: Springdale AR. 1989.

Riffel, Brent E., "Prohibition," *The Encyclopedia of Arkansas History and Culture*. http://encyclopediaofarkansas.net (accessed 2004)

Shaw, Robert B. "History of the Comstock Patent Medicine Business and Dr. Morse's Indian Root Pills." http://www.fullbooks.com/History-of-the-Comstock-Patent-Medicine.html (accessed 2004)

Young, James Harvey "Chapter 9: St. George and the Dragon," *The Toadstool Millionaires: A Social History of Patent Medicines in America before Federal regulation*. Princeton University Press 1961. http://www.quackwatch.com (accessed 2004)

175 Years of Groceries

The Grocery Business in Fayetteville, Arkansas

Before John William Campbell moved his family to Fayetteville, Arkansas, from White County, Arkansas in 1918, his small country store near Roosevelt sold "everything from horse collars to brown sugar," according to his son. He and his family lived next to the store, first in a log cabin and then in a small frame house he built. Once in Fayetteville, forty-year-old John William opened for business at the southeast corner of Rock and Mill to sell groceries and second hand goods. He traded—among other things—guns, horses, automobiles, and parcels of land. It is believed that throughout the next thirteen years, in spite of Prohibition, a suitably persuasive individual might find John William knowledgeable as to the whereabouts of bootleg whiskey.

With the profits of his enterprise, John William raised a family of seven children in a comfortable home and provided college education for those who pursued it. In spite of a fourth grade education, his skill with numbers and a natural talent for trade served him well in building a viable, rewarding career. The talents of his chosen vocation were passed on to his children; of four sons, three would establish grocery stores in Fayetteville. For a short time, one daughter and her husband would also own and operate a Fayetteville grocery, while a second daughter and her husband would clerk in one.

From the time of the first settlements, Americans had depended on the "keeper of stores" to provide everything they might need and couldn't produce themselves including exotics like coffee, spices, and sugar. Folks of lesser means might make-do with sorghum molasses instead of sugar and chicory instead of coffee, but sooner or later a trip to the country store would be necessary even if only for nails or cinnamon. Rural grocers generally sprang from the ranks of boys "who didn't have a farm to work on, preachers', lawyers', and doctors' sons."[2]

J.W. Campbell family 1918.
Left to right: John Carl, J.W., Ruby, Ruth "Dink," wife Mary, Evertt, and Zenola "Nodi." Oldest son Zach and youngest son Russell not shown.

John William fit this mold. His storekeeping benefitted from what he had learned in childhood travels as his father preached in east Arkansas and western Tennessee. John William knew what goods people needed and how to obtain and sell such goods in the most profitable manner. His store modeled the rural standard. Post offices were commonly located in the store, and the storekeeper frequently served as a kind of banker of valued goods and/or money between third parties. Fresh produce and animal products from the family farm could be traded for rope, nails, or tobacco. Credit accounts allowed for the spring purchase of flour or salt to be charged against the expected proceeds of a fall harvest.

Supplies for country stores often traveled long and tortured routes to reach their destination. Laborious wagon journeys or river transport brought large wooden barrels of goods such as pickles or crackers, which were then rolled into the store to be parceled out

---

[2] Carson, Gerald, *The Old Country Store*. NY: Oxford University Press. 1954 p 34

according to the customer's need. [The familiar wood-stave barrel ranged in capacity from 63 to 114 gallons and led to phrases such as "cracker barrel sage," referring to those who frequented the country store to expound on topics of the day, and "cash on the barrelhead," meaning to pay for goods immediately.] Such methods did not necessarily incorporate sanitation or standardized pricing.

The first Congressional effort to ensure food safety occurred in 1883 with the passage of the United States Tea Adulteration Act, a response to growing concern about contamination of this popular product. In 1899, the National Biscuit Company (NaBisCo) "invented" individual packaging for their crackers, touting improved quality in terms of crispness and sanitation. Six years later, Upton Sinclair published *The Jungle*, a scathing expose of the meat packing industry in Chicago. Within a few months, Congress passed the Meat Packing Act and the Pure Food and Drug Act, heralding a new era in consumer protection.

As concerns over packaging and sanitation grew, the rural grocery trade saw changes brought about not only by purity standards but also the railroad, automobile, manufacturing methods, and the growth of urban America. The bulk of this change occurred between the 1880s and the 1920s during the peak of John William's business years. The old country store began to vanish.

Fayetteville's earliest grocery opened in 1830 just two years after the first settlers arrived. Prior to this, settlers made laborious wagon journeys to Cane Hill or Evansville to obtain necessary goods. This enterprise under the ownership of John Nye was located on the west side of the Square, although at the time, the Square had not yet taken shape, and the location was simply described as alongside the road to "Evansville country."

The Place and the Articles!!!

Liles & Thomas,

SELL the best family supplies—the sourest Vinegar, sweetest Molasses, the purest Wines and Liquors, the pleasantest Cigars, the cleanest Rice; in fact, the best of every thing.

Their stock comprises articles too numerous to mention. The leading articles used by the public, we offer at the lowest prices, such as tobacco of many varieties; coffee and sugar of the best quality; Teas, fresh and unadulterated; carefully baked Soda Crackers.

Confectionery.

CANDIES, fresh and of every fanciful stripe and hue; Almonds, cream nuts; ground peas, commonly known as goobers; filberts, new raisins; strong pepper, black and red; soda and saleratus; allspice, candles, ginger, etc., etc.

Liquors.

COGNAC and American brandies, Bourbon and all the celebrated brands of Cincinnati whiskies, Geneva, pure claret, sweet wine, port wine, Malaga, Teneriffe, Madeira and

Champagne Wines!

NEW ARK CIDER, cherry bounce, brandy cherries, cordials, etc., etc.

Mackerel, Scotch Herring, Sardines, lobsters, and fresh fat Oysters, hermetically sealed and prepared for immediate use; pickles, pigs feet, picolilly preserves and and condiments; ginger, race and ground, nutmegs, cloves, and every variety of delicacies for table use. Our stock is well assorted and particularly adapted to wants of the citizens of this city and vicinity. Our prices are low and as we believe in quick sales and small profits, we hope for the continued patronage of our old customers, and the opportunity of giving satisfaction to the new.   LILES & THOMAS,
Sept. 22.—4   West side Public Square.

According to a 1993 article in the *Northwest Arkansas Times*, "Nye's store was built of black oak poles. It had no floor. The building was covered with boards riven from a great oak felled just below the spring south of what was later the Frisco train depot on Dickson Street."[3]

With the passing of another ten years and the state's admission to statehood in 1836, Fayetteville became home to "six dry-goods stores, three blacksmiths, two wagon shops, a saddlery shop," a cabinetmaker maker, and "in 1845, the first beef market opened and sold steak at three cents and roasts at two-and-a-half cents a pound. Salesmen stayed at the Byrnside House or the City Hotel and cleared the dust from their throats at William

---

[3]"First Store Opens in Fayetteville Around 1830" Times Staff, *Northwest Arkansas Times* Pg 1 Looking Back, Wednesday July 28, 1993. Courtesy Shiloh Museum.

McGarrah's saloon at the back of his grocery store."[4]

By 1850, newspaper advertisements hawked local wares and became a chronicle of the local grocery trade. The 1853-55 editions of Fayetteville's *South-West Independent* included grocery ads, even though at this time the term "grocer" carried a tawdry connotation related to the alcohol trade. Foodstuffs were but one line of stock among the wide array of items made available by merchants of those times. Liles & Thomas, located on the west side of the Fayetteville Square, offered "the best family supplies—the sourest Vinegar, the sweetest Molasses, the purest Wines and Liquors, the pleasantest Cigars, the cleanest Rice; in fact, the best of everything." L. B. Cunningham "did business in a two-story frame house on the corner..." Stirman & Dickson "sold goods in a brick store-house." W. M. Black took over the place of Bishop & Boyer, and W. A. Watson managed a store for Baker & Bishop of Van Buren.[5] J. C. Hodges owned and operated Fayetteville Family Supply Store (west side next to

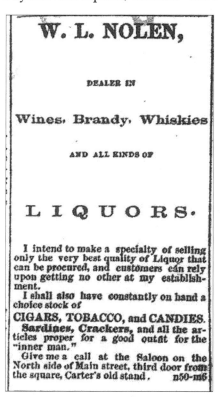

---

[4]"Town 'admirably situated on beautiful eminence'" by Jill M. Rohrbach, *Morning News* Mar 1, 1999, citing Kent R. Brown "A Timeless Epoch ... in Harmony with Ozark heritage."
[5]"Fayetteville 30 Years Ago, As Told in 1882," by J. Dickson Black, *The Northwest Arkansas Merchandiser* Wednesday September 8, 1976. Citing J. H. Van Hoose. Courtesy Shiloh Museum

Washington House).

Following the Civil War, pages of the *Fayetteville Weekly Democrat* ran a few ads such as G. W. Little's in 1869: "Beef! Beef! Beef! Fresh beef every morning at the new Market house, west side of the public square in the McCombs building.

I will sell beef cheaper than any market house in the city." But the community's larger merchants hosted the bulk of grocery advertisement, which included notice of liquor, confectioneries, nails, rope, iron, yarn, boots, and drugs, among other things. Other businesses selling edibles included Blackwell and Bros. (northwest corner of Square) and W. L. Nolen (a saloon on the north side of Main Street, 3rd door from the Square).

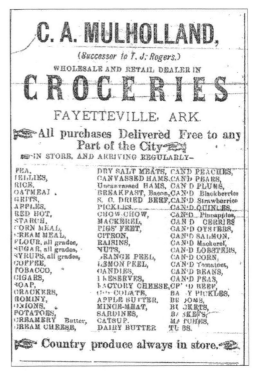

August 1869

In the 1870s, grocery trade involved W. M. Bozarth, Baum & Brothers, Robards & Morrison (north side, Trott's old stand), P. McGreevy (north side), A. C. Bowers (confectionery), C. Jackson & Co. (opened in 1872 in the "new brick," west side; succeeded by Evers &

Jackson), John L. Blakely (south side), and George P. Horton (new brick, west side, advertising that "J. C. Massie will be found").

In the 1880 *Fayetteville Democrat*, advertisements by T. J. Rogers promoted his business as wholesale and retail dealer in "staple and fancy groceries," housed "in the Jackson Brick, West Side the Public Square." Among the goods available at T. J. Rogers were tea, dry salt meats, crackers, and canned goods. C. A. Mulholland took over this enterprise by 1881 and faced a new competitor, Gray & Tunstill, who advertised a "complete line of groceries of every description" at their "first-class grocery establishment in the new McIlroy Building, East Side Public Square."

The 1882 opening of the railroad through Fayetteville brought new merchants and shoppers. That year M. W. Dorman advertised as "dealer in Groceries, Provisions, Canned Goods, Confectioneries, Cigars, Tobacco," with "Fresh Bread, Cakes, and Pies always on hand." Customers were advised to "give me a call at the Rock House on Center Street, three doors east the Post-office." Mr. Dorman's enterprise also included

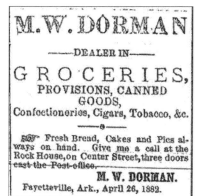

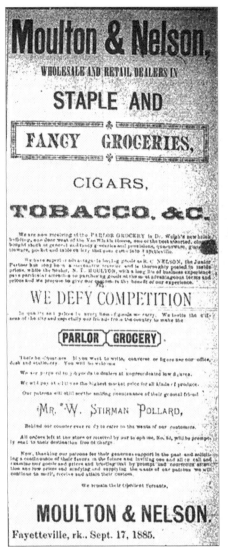

"Marble Works, Bakery, and Restaurant," with "all work in this line [of marble] done with neatness and dispatch and as cheap as at any other works west of St. Louis."

Advertisement by the City Meat Market under Reuben Carte, Proprietor, offered "the choicest meats the country affords."

Mulholland & White, Northeast Corner Public Square (the so-called Van Hoose Corner), announced the formation of their partnership to deal in staple and fancy groceries and solicited trade in "wheat, hides, furs, dried fruit, and country produce of all kinds." Moulton & Nelson sold goods at Dr. Welsh's new brick one door west of Van Winkle house, and included the Parlor Grocery. Another 1880s grocery was Wilson and Dickson (not known if this is the same Dickson or the son of Dickson who partnered 30 years earlier in Stirman & Dickson).

L. B. Lantrip opened his confectionery concern in 1884 and by 1888 had joined with A. H. Miller in a grocery establishment.

In Fayetteville's listings in R. L. Polk and Co.'s *Arkansas State Gazetteer and Business Directory* of 1884-5, there were three meat markets, four grocers, one confectioner, and one produce dealer. These were not complete listings, however, since some of the firms advertising in the local newspaper of those years were not among those named in the *Gazetteer*.

Subsequent Gazetteer editions reflected the growth of the region. In 1888-9, there were two meat markets and three confectioners along with ten grocers. In 1892-3, there were two meat markets, four confectioners, and seventeen grocers.

In the 1898-9 edition, there were three meat markets, two confectioners, and fifteen grocers, and about this time Polk began publishing a business directory just for Fayetteville.

At the turn of the century as John William built his rural grocery business in east Arkansas, Fayetteville hosted a population of 6000 people with 34 establishments selling groceries, meat, produce, confections, and similar goods (1 market per 176 people).

The growth of the trade reflected the growth of the city population. Virtually all citizens lacked motorized transportation and the majority of grocery shopping among city dwellers was conducted by foot travel. Of necessity, grocery markets were within ready distance to most homes so that a child might be sent running for a last-minute purchase of baking powders.

In 1904, downtown purveyors of grocery stock, fresh produce, or meat concentrated along the south side of the Square including Simpson, Ladd & Co. produce at 7 East Mountain, J. S. Lackey Produce Co. at 11 E. Mountain and Lackey groceries at 15 E. Mountain, C. C. Conner at 1-3 West Mountain, Lantrip & Miller at 7 W. Mountain, Ashby Grocer Co. at 9 W. Mountain, McHenry & Bryan Produce at 110-112 W. Mountain, and Fayetteville Produce Co. at 115 W. Mountain.

On the north side of the Square in 1900, D. M. Harbison sold meat at 4 E. Center as did G. W. Hurst at 12

1904

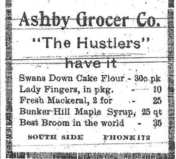

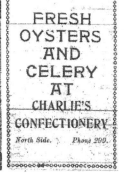

W. Center and J. F. Johnson at 18 N. Block. Sneed Brothers manufactured and retailed candy at 3 S. Block. Other confectioneries selling candies, cigars, and newspapers at the Square were George H. Stapp at 10 W. Center and E. Wilson at 6 E. Center. Gilbreath & Taylor sold groceries at 8 E. Center, while A. C. Hamilton & Co. conducted their grocery trade at 112-114 W. Center.

Twenty years later, about the time of John William's arrival, grocery trade at the Square had consolidated to a smaller number of businesses. J. C. Reese was selling groceries at 3 East Mountain and A. H. Miller remained at 7 W. Mountain, where he sold groceries and wholesaled for Fayetteville Poultry & Eggs. He also had a market, Miller & Son, around the corner at 180 E. Rock Street. The rest of the Mountain Street markets were gone. A new grocer, H. L. Harris, was open for business on the east side of the square at 18 S. East.

Moore Cash Grocery had opened at 6 East Center, advertising as "The Busy Store – groceries, flour and feed." Gilbreath & Taylor's old location at 8 E. Center had become Fuller's Sanitary Meat Market (1920 ad: "We operate our own cold storage.") and Long's Meat Market had opened at 14 E. Center (Ad: "Handles the Best of Fresh and Cured Meats at all Times. Buyers and Shippers of Live Stock.") "A E F" Confectionery had opened for business at 17 N. Block with "homemade candy and cream daily. All kinds of

Saturday at
Square Deal
Grocery
329 S. School St.   Phone 48

50 lbs Aristos Flour	$2.10
50 lbs Polar Bear Flour	$2.10
50 lbs Kansas Boy	$2.00
50 lbs Bouquet Flour	$1.85
25 lbs Cotton Queen	85c
10 lbs Crusto Lard	$1.15
3 large cans Home Packed Tomatoes	25c
4 cans Pork & Beans	25c
3 cans Peas	25c
4 cans Mince Meat	25c
4 lbs Black Eye Peas	25c
3 lbs Good Coffee	25c
3 lbs Calif. Dried Peaches	25c
10 bars good Soap	25c
3 pkgs Corn Flakes	25c

Sugar at Cost With Other Groceries.

Best Goods—Lowest Possible Prices—Courteous Treatment.

QUICK DELIVERIES
A Trial Order Will Convince You.

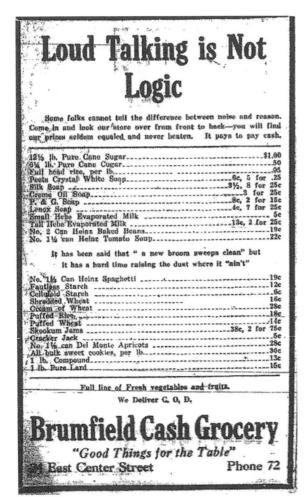

sweets."

T. J. Boyd was selling groceries at 123 W. Center. Smelser & Eason provided flour and feed at 119 W. Center competing with the flour and feed sales of Farmer's Exchange at 15 N. Block. Goddard Grocer Company, a wholesaler, advertised: "We stand behind 'Marine Club,' 'Festal Hall,' 'Sweet Home' brands of pure food. 'Sugar Loaf' fancy canned vegetables when you want the best."

On the west side of the Square, C. O. Hansard sold "groceries, glassware, and queensware."

Due to its proximity to the University as well as the railroad, Dickson Street served as its own center of commerce in the flow of Fayetteville's business. In 1904, Lester & Son grocery was located at 316 W. Dickson, McCormick & Son meat market at 320 W. Dickson, McClanahan & Williams grocery at 402 W. Dickson, W. E. Dowell meat market at 408 W. Dickson, William Lilly confectioners at 414 W. Dickson, Bates Brothers groceries at 430 W.

Dickson, Lewis & Sharp grocers at 521 W. Dickson, and at the corner of West and Meadow, George H. Askew managed the Hammond Packing Company which sold meat over the counter.

Twenty years later on Dickson Street, Star Grocery had replaced Lester & Son at 316 W. Dickson and next door was the new City Bakery, John W. Seamster proprietor of the wholesale and retail enterprise. Their city directory ad states: "We specialize in cakes and cream bread." McCormick & Son was gone, as was McClanahan & Williams, but across the street J. F. Winchester had opened his new grocery at 401 W. Dickson. E. C. Gollaher sold groceries at 414 W. Dickson and Bates Brothers had expanded. A new concern at 520 W. Dickson, Champion News

FISH! ✢ FISH!

Special drive in family white fish, nice, medium size lake whit fish, 4 lbs 25c
Big greden bloaters, each 5c.

Oranges, nice California navels, per doz 15c.
English walnuts, soft shell new crop, this sale 3 lbs 50c.
Fancy cooking figs, 3 lbs 25c.
Prunes, very large, lb 12½.
Raisins, loose muscatels, 12½c value, lb 10c, 3 for 25c.
Raisins, package, seeded, a bargain, 2 pkgs 15c.
Apples, country dried, quarters, lb 10c.
Apricotts, fanciest evaporated, lb 15c.
Peaches, extra large, fancy evaporated, 2 lbs 25c.
Choice dates, 3 lbs 25c.
Stuffed Olives, good quality, a bargain, per bottle 10c
Salmon, we save you two to five cents a can on salmon.
25c buckeye 20c.
15c pink 10c.
Good red, 2 for 25c.
Rice is higher but we still offer that fancy head Japan, 4 lbs for 25c; 18 lbs $1.00.
Hominy cracked corn, 8 lbs 25c.
Hominy, flaked, 6½ lbs 25c.
One of our customers was asked 5c lb for this at another store, or 30 per cent more than our price. Note how such bargains will help your dollars stretch.
Choice navy beans, 5 lbs 28c.
Best pink beans, 5 lbs 28c.
Big gallon can pie peaches, fine stock, only 25c. Per doz. $2.85.
Fancy Elbertas in syrup, per can 14c; doz $1.65.
20c home canned pears, out to 15c can.
Canned apples, fine stock, 9c: 3 for 25c.
20c California apricotts,

cut to can 15c.
Choice canned blackberries, 3 for 25c.
Apple butter, Heinz, can 15c.
Peas, beauty brand, worth 15c for 12c.
Peas, early June, 10c; 3 for 28c.
Tomatoes, best can, 8c; doz 95c.
Corn, choice Iowa, 9c: 3 for 25c.
4 cans string beans 25c.
2 cans succotash 25c.
2 cans okra 25c.
3 cans red kidney beans 25c.
Banner oats, pkg 29c.
Scotch Quaker, pkg 11c.
Postum, pkg 23c.
Hams, Calumet, choice quality, lb 12½c.
Cottolene, 10 lb pail $1.30.
Good oil, 5 gal 60c.
Best oil, gal 17c; 5 gal 80c
Lenox soap 4c, 7 for 25c.
Starch, best bulk, 4 lbs 25c.
Potatoes, Colorado, pk 35c
Bakers' chocolate, ¼ lb 10c lb 40c.
30c Lowney's cocoa, can 23c.
Soda, guaranteed quality, six 1 lb pkgs 25c.
50c can Karo syrup 45c.
Coffee is up about 2 cents; some say 2½c; we still sell at the old price, good Rio, 15c lb; 8 lbs for $1.
Choice Rio 15c lb; 7 lbs $1.
25c sunshine brand per lb 20c.
Onion sets—yellow and red bellows, Northern grown qt 10c.
Best cane granulated sugar. With $3.50 orders for other groceries, 18½ lbs $1; with $5 order other groceries, 20 lbs $1.

McGUIRE'S
CASH GROCERY
North Side Square   Phone 444

Company, sold Elmer's and Lowrey Box Candies, magazines, stationery, newspapers, candies, tobacco, and cigars.

The several blocks bordering the railroad tracks at Dickson were the site of primarily wholesale food business. In 1900, along Gregg St. where it used to travel south from Dickson Street, J. H. Stanley managed Armour & Co. meat operation while J. H. Williams sold flour and feed at the same location. Fayetteville Roller Mills and John P. Scott sold flour and feed at 335 N. West. By 1920, at the corner of West and Spring, McHenry & Bryan wholesaled and retailed poultry, eggs, and dairy products (Ad: "Oldest poultry house in the state. Specialty – Poultry and Eggs in Car Lots. Phones Local 201; L. D. 1801").

One block west Jay Fulbright oversaw operations of Ozark Poultry and Egg Company. Meat packing, poultry/egg, dairy, produce, feed/flour milling, canning operations, and massive wholesale food shipping operations at the railway station occupied much of the available space between 1900 and 1950 including H. Rouw Co. produce, Champion fruit, Lewis & Sharp grocers, J. H. Williams flour and feed, Hammond Packing Company, McHenry & Bryan (poultry, eggs, dairy, became Ozark Poultry & Egg Co.), T. K. Taylor meats, Williams Produce, Campbell Soup, and Jerpe Dairy Products Corporation.

The neighborhoods north of the University had only one grocery in 1904, an establishment operated by Algy (sic) Moore at Leverett near York (now Cleveland).

To the east of the Square in 1900, O. C. Cate offered provisions at 2 N. College. Flour and feed was sold by Dry & Welsh and Fayetteville Feed & Fuel at 14 N. College, and also by City Roller Mills and D. Portnell (miller) at Mill near Rock. Nearby grocers were at 3 Mill St., a store operated by Cal H. Clark, and Freeman Brothers Grocery at Mill and Ash (Arthur J. and Harry E.

Freeman). It was in this area that John William established his second hand store in 1918. Local milling operations ceased by the 1920s, leaving the J. W. Skelton grocery market at 222 Mill (1920), Fred Brooks grocer at or near that location (1929), and Harvey L. Harris, Huntsville Road (1929).

South-lying establishments in 1904 included M. T. Crippen at 321 S. School, E. C. Harrison at 338 S. School, R. S. Black and B. Mitchell both with stores on Cemetery Road near Wall (Quicktown area). Bentley & Keeler sold groceries and other goods and hosted the Vale Post Office at Fayette Junction, Fayetteville's first suburb which was not then within the city limits. (The market was at the corner of Vale and Cato Springs Road.) By 1920, considerable growth had taken place in south Fayetteville. There were H. C. King at 329 S. School, C. C. Rough at 400 S. School, and J. B. Clarke at 420 S. School. G. W. Barnes and Berl Dodd had stores on the Prairie Grove Road (now 6th Street), while Quicktown hosted D. E. Hammontree at 412 Cemetery (now called Government Avenue), Algie Moore (relocated from his first store at Leverett and York) at 425 Cemetery, and G. F. Puterbaugh at 428 Cemetery (now the location of a cabinet shop). Hammontree advertised "groceries, flour, feed, hardware, and general merchandise." The Fayette Junction area was served by H. F. Allen grocers at the Parksdale Addition (15th St. and Brooks) and Bland & Webb at Vale and Cato Springs Road.

Outlying grocers by the 1920s included four in the area north of the University campus: Square Deal Grocery, 634 N. Leverett established circa 1926; Reep's Grocery 713 N. Leverett established before 1920; J. W. Murphy, 804 N. Leverett, established before 1920; and Richard A. Jeffery, 812 N. Leverett, taking over the store location along York established before 1904 by Algie Moore.

Out the north highway (U. S. 71) at 900 N. College, Menges Cash

Grocery had opened for business by 1929, and to the east at the southeast intersection of Maple and Olive, R. L. Brown had opened a small grocery by 1920.

Back in White County, John William's enterprise had been the only show in town. He recruited help from his cousin Wesley Monroe Campbell who, according to family history, "hauled groceries from Searcy, wholesale, and Bald Knob and around that way and made about two trips a week for groceries." Now in Fayetteville, he faced well established competition with sophisticated wholesaling operations. John William decided to include second hand goods with his grocery stock and other items on the side. Only four second-hand stores were open for business in 1918 and like the soon-to-fade general stores and mercantiles, these establishments sold a wide variety of goods. At the time he added his east Arkansas family to the 7,482 people already living in Fayetteville (1920 census), forty groceries, confectioneries, meat markets, and produce markets had established operations in or near Fayetteville (1 market per 187 people).

As the grocery trade changed and grew with Fayetteville, business opportunities were not missed by the Campbell family. By 1932, John William's oldest child Zachariah (age 33) had become the proprietor of a grocery at 713 N. Leverett, taking over Reep's Grocery and installing his little sister Ruth (age 20) and her husband Dick Bennett as clerks. The second Campbell son Evertt (age 29) and his wife Evalee (McCurdy) had established three groceries: Campbell's Cash Grocery #1 at 108 W. Center, Campbell's Cash Grocery #2 at 337 S. School (enlarged from Ideal Grocery established before 1929), and Campbell's Cash Grocery #3 at 39 E. South (established before 1929 by Bayless G. Lewis). Third son John Carl Campbell (age 24) and his new wife Opal

(Rutherford) had opened Rock Street Grocery at 223 S. Mill. Fifth child Ruby (age 22) and her husband Cecil R. Bennett opened Snappy Service Grocery at 318 West Dickson.

The Campbell siblings entered a challenging business climate during the 1930s Depression years. The same number of groceries—fourteen—operated around the Square as had been there in 1904, but another 45 stores elsewhere in the community serviced over 10,500 in population. There was now one market per 178 people and with use of the increasingly available automobile, shoppers were more likely to shop around to compare prices.

The 1935 scene included Cox's Market occupying a stretch of West Mountain that faced the Square from the south. Sav-It Grocery operated on the east side. Just to the south of the Square on East Avenue was Hammond Produce. Along Center Street between the Square and the courthouse, H. G. Ward butchered fresh cuts at 8 E. Center, with neighbors Central Food Market at 30 E. Center and Economy Grocery at 32 E. Center. City Grocery with proprietors T. J. Conner and H. K. Bogert held on at 6 E. Center advertising "Good Things to Eat. We Solicit a Share of Your Trade. On Smokey Row."

The 19th century development of the term "Smokey Row" has been explained variously as resulting from the close proximity of buildings which heated with wood or coal and thus produced a lot of smoke, or possibly the clustering of cigar-

PIGGLY WIGGLY
HELPS THOSE WHO HELP THEMSELVES

Del Monte Week Mar. 15th to 21st

We Have Them--Look at the Prices

No. 2½ Sliced Y. C. Peaches	30c
No. 2½ Melba Halves Peaches	24c
No. 2 White Cling Peaches	30c
No. 2½ Crushed Pineapple	29c
No. 2 Royal Ann Cherries	34c
No. 2 Fresh Lima Beans	32c
No. 2½ Spinach	22c
No. 2 Very Small Peas	28c
Tomato Sauce	9c
Asparagus Tips	41c

SPECIAL! SPECIAL!
Just received, full line of Heinz' 57 Varieties Vinegar, Beans and Tomato Products. You will never regret using the best.

Piggly Wiggly
North Side of Square
We Save You Money

puffing attorneys with their offices so near the courthouse. The position of the courthouse on the east end of the street would have largely blocked the normal exit of air pushed by prevailing west winds. There is, however, the likelihood that one or more grocers may have set up meat-smoking operations which would have kept low hickory fires smoldering as hams and bacon cured. All these elements occurring simultaneously would have layered a smoky pall over the street.

Along the north side of the Square were the new Fayetteville Piggly Wiggly and J. O. Mayes grocer, with Cowen Grocery at 27 N. Block. To the west of Campbell's Cash Grocery #1 at 108 W. Center was Guy T. Reed at 110 W. Center, the Farmers Market produce operation at 118 W. Center, and City Produce at 120 W. Center. Bob White Pastry Shop at the northeast corner of the Square offered "Delicious Pastries, Pies, Cakes, Rolls and Bread. Homemade Candy. House to House Delivery" (1939). Other groceries on streets near the Square were Alma Bohe's store at 123 W. Center and Miller & Son at 180 E. Rock. Steve's Place at 15 N. Block sold candies.

Cecil and Ruby Bennet's Snappy Service Grocery faced stiff competition for Dickson Street shoppers. Already there were the veteran grocers Bates Brothers, who had been selling groceries since before the turn of the century. King Food Market, started at 400 S. School by H. C. King, was now owned by Mrs. Olive D. King with Lloyd D. Cate as business partner at its new location on Dickson Street, first at 300 then 216 W. Dickson. Next door to Cecil and Ruby was Star Grocery at 316 W. Dickson, established before 1920. Winchester Cash Grocery & Market at 401 W. Dickson had also opened at least fifteen years earlier. At 408 W. Dickson, Supreme Food Market had taken over the old W. E. Dowell meat market location, another pre-1900 enterprise. Rouw Company flour and feed sales were located at 443 W. Dickson (now Walton Arts Center). Henry J. Dever operated a grocery at 352 N. West and Williams Produce Company was located at 410 W. Spring.

By 1939, Dickson Street operations of Snappy Service Grocery were handled by Ruby alone and by 1947, groceries were no longer sold at that location. King's Market yielded its first location to Goff Brothers where by 1955 Goff had opened Consumer's Market No. 2. Star Grocery became Pense's Grocery & Market by 1939, and then disappeared. Winchester's Market became Davidson's Food Store by 1947, and then disappeared. Supreme Food Market had become Kroger Grocery & Baking Company by 1939, but then it too did not continue. By 1955, Dickson Street was down to King's Food Market, the Goff Brothers' Consumers Market, and the venerable Bates Brothers Grocery.

Zach Campbell's Leverett Street Store continued at that location through 1955, although by 1939 it was under the management of Herman Stubblefield. By 1947, Enos Cupps ran the store. Other 1935 competitors just one block north of Campbell included J. W. Murphy, who had started his grocery at 804 N. Leverett by 1920; subsequent owners at this location were Julius Lehman in 1947 and Tru-Val-U Food Market by 1955. At 810 N. Leverett, Richard A Jeffery also ran a grocery he had begun by 1920 (758 W. York) and expanded into 812 N. Leverett by 1955. Other competitors for the University trade north of campus included James F. Ladd, who had taken over the 1929 Golden Rule Grocery at 529 Whitham, and Mrs. Seth Pennock, who had continued her husband's 1929 establishment at 680 Storer (1112 W. York). Ralph W. Tapp had become the new proprietor at 541 N. Garland, a location first listed in the 1929-30 directory under the ownership of Thos. A. Matthews. Mr. Tapp would continue at this place at least through 1939.

In addition to his Leverett Street operation, Zach Campbell built a new store at 525 Mission in an area just north of established grocery businesses. He lived in an adjacent apartment with his wife Sylvia (Davis). Since before 1920, when Joseph S. Holcomb purveyed his wares at 424 Mission, established Mission Street markets had included Gus F. Schwartz who either moved or expanded to 440 N. Mission by 1939. The vicinity was favorable, evidently, since Bert Dorman had a grocery at 437 Mission in 1947 and Clawson's Grocery at 438 Mission helped supply the neighborhood in 1955, probably taking over the Schwartz enterprise (southeast corner Mission and Maple). One block west was the long successful grocery at the corner of Maple and Olive, first operated by R. L. Brown (1920), then as Graham Grocery and Market (1935–39), and then as Meistrell's Grocery (1955). The native stone building remains, occupied by an accounting firm. Mr. Brown took his grocery skills closer to town to build the Lafayette Grocery at 111 W. Lafayette, a place made famous in its robbery by Bonnie & Clyde's gang. Mr. Brown's red brick Lafayette Grocery building had ceased the grocery trade by 1947, but remained in various use until it was demolished in 2003 by Central United Methodist Church.

A block north of Zach's fine new store on Mission, East Side Service Station sold groceries as early as 1929, taken over by Herman Stubblefield by 1935 and then closed. Zach and Sylvia also operated a café on the southeast corner of the Huntsville Square, but after his mother's death early in 1937 and Sylvia's death in the spring of 1938, Zach sold his holdings to his brother Evertt and moved to Los Angeles California, where he died in 1958. Evertt took over ownership at Zach's Mission Street Store for some time, but by 1947, the store had been sold to Earl A. Sherry. It was named Gray's Grocery by 1955, and Phillips Mission Street Grocery in 1961. Grocery operations ceased sometime in the early

1980s. Today the remodeled building hosts an antique and home decor business.

One area that escaped the Campbell family's merchandising skills was the expansion of Fayetteville's growth to the north along College Avenue, where burgeoning population supported the New Park Grocery at 701 N. College by 1935. Named Park Cash Grocery in 1939, the establishment came under new ownership by 1955, then named Phillips Grocery, but did not survive to 1961 (probably the same Phillips as the Mission Street store). Located at the northwest corner of College and Rebecca, it may have been demolished as College Avenue was widened to accommodate increasingly heavy traffic along this section of Highway 71. By 1955, Safeway Stores had built a state-of-the-art supermarket at 612 N. College (current site of a skating rink), effectively sounding a death knell not only for Phillips' North College grocery but also for other smaller groceries to the north.

In 1920 W. D. Pearson had been selling groceries at 808 N. College, a location under the ownership of Frank Wilkins by 1947. Circa 1939, Harry B. Milligan ran a grocery and meat market at 816 N. College but no further listings occur for this address. By 1927 grocery sales were underway at 900 N. College first as Menges Cash Grocery, then owned by Clayton M. Davis by 1935. Subsequent owners were Edwin D. Forbes by 1939 and Earl Land by 1947, and the store remained under Land's ownership in 1955 as Land's Grocery. Today this building hosts a window tinting service. Other groceries clustered around this successful enterprise: Matthew I. Pearson at 912 N. College in 1929; J. W. Rowden at 901 N. College, 1935; and Davis Grocery at 902 N. College, 1939. Dixie Cream Shop was briefly located along this stretch of highway (1951) as was Edw. I. Troeger's confectionery store at 700 N. College.

While Safeway's new store was the nearest competitor to these smaller grocers, it was not alone. By 1961 a new IGA Thriftway Super Market had opened at 405 N. College (current site of an auto parts store) and a new Fairway Store Inc. had opened in Fayetteville's first shopping center—Evelyn Hills—at 1304 N. College. Still farther north, at the southeast corner of College and Sycamore, Botts Speedway Foods Inc. had opened store #14 at 1680 N. College (recently demolished).

Growth came to the south of town as well and this was the area where the Campbell grocery business thrived. Evertt's first store at 108 W. Center did not long remain in his hands. He sold the location to Piggly Wiggly by 1939 and used the profits to expand his venture at 337 S. School where he added a motel/rooms-for-rent wing built of native stone. The October 18-19, 1940 Campbell's Super Market grand opening was featured in an eight-page special section of the *Northwest Arkansas Times*. Photographs of Everett and Evalee bracket a photo of the new store front, while further down on the page are photos of the entire store personnel (thirteen men), of the new refrigerated meat counter, and of the modern-style grocery carts.

Featured text illustrates the new world of grocery trade, now very different from the country store of Evertt's father where customers would expect to pick up mail, trade milk for flour, or purchase nails:

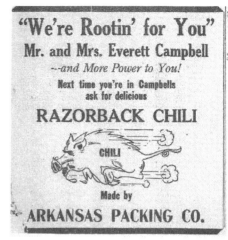

> Campbell's salutes the progress of Fayetteville. Campbell's hail the growth of Fayetteville, is proud to contribute its share toward bringing more of the fine things of life to the rapidly expanding population of this great community.
>
> As evidence of our faith we have now completed a vast new market which we honestly believe to be one of the finest food stores in the entire northwest of the state.
>
> This store is located for your greatest shopping convenience. It is planned and equipped in every way to make your marketing a pleasure. It is stocked-to-bursting with regular everyday necessities including famous nationally advertised brands, at everyday low prices. In addition, you will find here a rare collection of fancy packaged foods and fresh fruits and vegetables to meet the demands of the most discriminating tastes.
>
> You are cordially invited to

attend the grand opening of the New Campbell's Super Market Friday and Saturday. Hot coffee served free all day Saturday.

Multiple ads featuring congratulations to the new store and its owners are sponsored by Abshier-Bryan Motor Co., McIlroy Bank and Trust Co., Eason & Co. Insurance, Arkansas Western Gas Co., and an array of concerns who no doubt served as suppliers and equippers to the store including Royal Crown Bottling Co. (Nehi Beverages), Roberts Fixture Co. of Ft. Smith (Frigidaire Refrigeration and Hobart-Dayton Scales), Banfield Bros. Packing Co. (Sweetheart Products), White Diary Products of Ft. Smith (ice cream), Ozark Grocer Co., Fayetteville Milk Co., Dr. Pepper Bottling Co., Arkansas Packing Co. (Razorback Chili), Harris Baking Co., Wilson and Co. (Ideal Dog Food), and Cudahy Packing Co. (Puritan brand ham, bacon, lard). Other ads were sponsored by companies most likely involved in the construction of the new store, including Ft. Smith Structural Steel Company and Kelley Brothers Lumber Company.

The feature article about the store states:

> Campbell's Super Market No. 1...has been enlarged, remodeled and refinished. With complete new stock it will hold a formal opening starting Friday at 8 am and continuing all next week.

> Construction work has been underway for several months while business of the store has been carried on without interruption.

> Owned and operated by Mr. and Mrs. Evertt E. Campbell, local grocers, in business in the city or the vicinity for the past 12 years, the store draws business to Fayetteville from a trade territory of more than 30 miles in all directions.

The new building is constructed of native stone. All materials used were purchased locally and only local labor was used. All merchandise sold in the store, also is locally purchased and the business offers a large market. The super market, with its two branches also within the city, employs more than 15 persons giving support to approximately that many families.

Floor space is now 75 x 75 feet, according three times the display space as was had formerly. A complete line of groceries is carried, in addition to fresh meats and fruits and vegetables. Grains and feed are also stocked.

There is a full cement floor. The ceiling, above 12 foot walls, is of cellotex. New fluorescent light fixtures have been installed. The woodwork is natural colored veneer, contrasting with cream walls above which are four large ceiling-top windows to the north, flood-lighting the goods and floor below, and from the inside, affording a view to shoppers of a flower garden to the north, and now a riot of bloom.

The building is heated by gas, equipment for which also provides the cooling system in summer. In addition there are seven large ceiling fans that operating 12 hours a day prevent entrance in the store of flies or other insects.

The 75 foot front has new accordion glass doors that when pushed back expose the entire interior and its stock to the view of the passerby.

Display shelves are different from any previously installed in any store and were designed by Mrs. Campbell. They provide a maximum of display space and "reach-convenience," while taking up a minimum of room. The wall cases for cereals are of the slant type so designed that removal of a bottom box allows the space to be filled automatically by the box above, without handling or displacement.

Push cart gliders with rubber tires have been provided for customers which gives easy shopping convenience.

Goods are conveniently and expertly placed. The entire north side is allotted to cereals and canned goods. The south side is given over to the market, and fresh fruits and vegetables. Staples occupy the center. A portion of the space is allotted to a large stock of the better grades of bulk candies.

A ladies and children's rest room with all modern conveniences except hot water is provided for customers and the general public.

The business office is located in a balcony overlooking the entire store.

Yet to be placed also are upright post-mirrors and a super-outside sign, expected to extend entirely across the 75 foot building frontage, which also is spotlighted by tall lights already in place.

The Super Market has two branches, Store No. 2 located corner Mission and Gunter streets and managed by Alfred Anglin, and Store No. 3 on South College and managed by G. H. Hanna. They also are conducted on a cash basis. All three stores bulk of trade is of the cash and carry type.

R. E. Stewart is manager of the Super Market and has been employed in that capacity since the store opened 10 years ago. Aubrey Jones is manager of the meat department.

Mr. Campbell is son of J. W. Campbell, who also was in the grocery business here at one time. His first grocery experience was in his father's store located on the same street where his own market now is. His own first business was operated on Highway 62 South outside of city limits.

He has lived here since early youth and most of his life except during a time he served with the U. S. Navy.

Evertt died in a car wreck in 1956 while helping a friend tow a vehicle from Missouri. The store continued through 1969 under his name. As of 2021, the building was occupied by a restaurant equipment supply company.

Evertt's South School grocery faced considerable neighborhood competition over the early years of his and Evalee's enthusiastic management. J. E. White's store at 400 S. School was sold to Charles W. Babcock by 1947. Across 6th Street to the south in the next block of School, J. B. Clark and Son continued their 1920 grocery operation (first at 420 S. School, then at 504 S. School) only to see the business become White's Grocery and Station by 1939. Other grocery competitors along this business stretch of

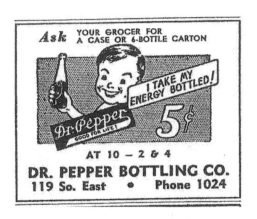

Highway 71 were J. C. White in 1929 at 611 S. School, Mrs. R. B. Armstrong in 1935 at 602 S. School, and John O. Curry at 605 S. School in 1947. Johnson & Son opened a store at 727 S. School by 1955. Further south along this highway were John D. Gibbs (Greenland Road, 1939 listing); Perry Grocery & Market (S. Hwy 71, 1955 listing); Botts Speedway Foods Inc. (1169 S. School, 1961 listing); and Purdy's Food Store (S. Hwy 71, 1961 listing).

Evertt's store #3 at 39 E. South was operating only as late as the

1939 city directory, yet the building remains standing today. One block to the west a more successful grocery established before 1929 as Lollar Grocery (15 W. South), was owned by Bill Williams by 1935 and operated as Williams & Williams Grocery in the 1939 directory, as Black & Son Grocery by 1955 and as Lancaster's Grocery in 1961. It is now the location of a water filter business. For a brief time, appearing only in the 1939 directory, Fred J. Rouse sold groceries at 303 W. South.

Another cluster of groceries sprang up along South College Avenue going south from the Washington County Courthouse. First known in the area was Glenwood Grocery at 614 S. College (by 1929), then Kay Davidson's venture at 700 S. College by 1935 after Jefferson School took over the east side of the 600 block. At some point, Evertt Campbell became the owner of this location; clearly he understood the site was well chosen. Subsequent management of Evertt's grocery sales at this store through 1961 included Mrs. Jimmie Parker (1939), and Harlan G. Hanna (1947 and up to 1970). College Street Grocery opened at 519 S. College in 1955 and became Johnson's Grocery in 1959. Johnson's Grocery remained open on weekday afternoons until 2004, offering a small line of groceries, candy, and tobacco. It is expected that with the closure of Jefferson Elementary School in 2004, grocery business here has forever ceased.

Outlying groceries were hardest hit by the increasing use of faster transportation and the development of super markets downtown. Between 1935 and 1955, stores in the Fairgrounds Addition (area of Razorback Road and 6th Street intersection) changed hands and then closed. Similarly, small markets in the Quicktown area (Prairie St., Government St.) vanished: of the five or more locations which sold groceries in this area over the first half of the century, only Charles Dealy's produce market at 423 Prairie remained as

1940s

late as 1961. Eli C. Mitchell's West Side Grocery at 142 S. Hill (northeast corner of Stone St.) ended operation by 1961. (The building was recently torn down to make way for a new apartment building parking lot, but the old steps up from the sidewalk remain.)

Markets along Sixth Street fared somewhat better: Charlie Jamison continued selling groceries along West 6th through 1961. Established in a log building as Wall Street Grocery by 1935, this building at 701 W. 6th has been torn down (southwest corner 6th and Hill) and a new gas station/convenience market has recently risen in the spot. J. F. Cowan and Ward's Grocery also remained along 6th Street until after 1961. Farther to the south, Oscar L. Harris continued the market at Vale and Cato Springs Road (demolished, later the site of Summercorn Foods into the 1990s) through 1961 and Kilgore Grocery continued to operate at 1540 Brooks Avenue until sometime in the 1960s.

Back at the Square, several locations persevered as grocery outlets for several decades until decentralization came fully to play by creating suburbs with their own shopping centers. While grocery trade throughout the 1800s seems to have been evenly distributed around the Square, by 1900, Mountain Street (south side of the Square) had become "grocery row." There, the longest-term grocery was at One West Mountain held by C. C. Conner in 1904 then by the Goff Brothers through the 1960s. The 1907 city directory names the Conner grocery men as C. C., T. J., and W. C.

The original rock building has been restored.

The Sav-It Grocery on the east side of the Square in 1935 was probably the same site as A. W. Karbe Grocery and Chas. P. Macey (both at 15 S. East in 1939) but it is not known where this was in relationship to the McIlroy Building mentioned in 1880s ads. All the structures facing the Square along East Avenue were demolished for the construction of First National Bank (now a complex of condominiums and commercial space).

Traveling west of the Square along Center Street, the 112– 120 W. Center area progressed from A. C. Hamilton & Company produce in 1904; Smelser & Eason flour/feed stores in 1920; and Farmers Market and City Produce in 1935 and through 1961. This area was subsumed in the 1970s by the First Federal Building (now E. J. Ball Plaza). Bohe's Grocery remained along the south side of this stretch of Center Street from before 1935 until sometime after 1947 (now a parking lot).

```
BOHE A
        GROCERIES
        FRESH MEATS
        VEGETABLES
     Feed - Flour - Notions
      "Service That Satisfies"
          — WE DELIVER —
     123 W Center..............566
```

Phone directory ad 1934, 1936

On the east side of the Square along East Center, 8 East Center was continuously occupied in grocery trade from Fayetteville's early days, from Gilbreath & Taylor in 1904, Fuller's Sanitary Meat Market in 1920, then Fuller's Market, H. G. Ward, Ward's Market and finally to Taylor's Grocery & Market in 1947. This entire section of Center Street is now occupied by the University of Arkansas Center for Continuing Education.

King Food Market at 300 W. Dickson then 216 W. Dickson remained in continuous activity from before 1935 through 1955, when it was taken over by the Goff Brothers and became

Consumers Market No. 2 by 1961. This is now part of the site of the so-called Three Sisters building. Groceries were sold at 401 W. Dickson from before 1920 until after 1939 by J. F. Winchester. By 1947 it was named Davidson's Food Store. It is now the site of the Walton Arts Center rose garden.

1940s

By far the longest term grocer along Dickson Street was Bates Brothers Grocery at the northeast corner of Dickson and West. In fact, Bates Brothers was Fayetteville's longest lived grocery in business at the same location and under the same name from the time it was opened by John Stephen Bates in 1897 until after 1961. The 1906 city directory names J. Steve and Joe R. Bates as the owner-operators. After 1912 when Steve went into business as the Mountain Top Fruit Farm, his younger brother Joseph Russell owned and operated the store. Other brothers and members of the Bates family worked in the store.

1909

Through the late 1960s and into the 1980s, the Bates Brothers grocery buildings became a series of bars, most famously The Swingin' Door. By the late 1980s, the deteriorating brick building sat vacant. In

the early 1990s, the structures at this location were extensively restored and remodeled to house Ozark Brewing Company, a micro-brewery and restaurant which closed in early summer 2004 and reopened that fall as Hog Haus Brewing Company. The entire structure has now been renovated into a nondescript red brick box.

Along West Avenue to the north of Dickson, Handy Grocery started at 352 N. West before 1929 and then moved to 651 W. Center where it took over Mrs. Laura Stiles' operation and continued after 1939 as "Andy Handy." Like Piggly Wiggly, Handy Andy was a nationally-advertised business name. It is not known if the local Andy Handy was affiliated or the owner merely borrowed and juggled the words. (The West Center address is now the site of apartments and parking.) Coming in behind Handy Grocery at 352 N. West was Henry J. Dever, who was still selling groceries at this location in 1947. By 1955 the business was named Hobbs Grocery. The tiny building remains today, home to a vintage clothing shop.

At the corner of School and Spring, or 322 W. Spring, Marshall Grocery was established by 1927 and remained in active grocery trade through 1947. Their advertisement in the 1927 directory: "We strive to please. Quality groceries—Service—Satisfaction. A clean store—a clean stock. Prompt service—a square deal." The 1939 directory ad: "We strive to please. Quality groceries. Fresh and cured meats. We deliver." In 1947, their ad simply states: "We strive to please." The building has remained in continuous service, for a while home to a hardware store and then providing shelter to a bicycle sales and service shop into the early 21st century.

North of the University campus, growth continued to push business districts outward. In addition to the cluster of food retailers on Leverett, groceries were sold at 529 Whitham from before 1929 until after 1961 (Burl M. Hankins 1947; Mac's Grocery 1955-57). This structure no longer exists, nor does the Storer Street location of Pennock's store.

To the west along Garland Avenue, Campus Food Store at 538 N. Garland lasted until after 1961 and Loren E. Vaughan ran his modest grocery store at 1023 W. Hughes from before 1939 until after 1961. The Vaughan building remains in use as a residence. Oak Plaza Shopping Center was built around 1970 and housed Dillon's, the first supermarket in this part of Fayetteville. Dillon's was supplanted in the early 1990s by Harp's at 1189 N. Garland. A grocery existed at 1001 N. Garland before 1935, when Loren Vaughan first entered the grocery scene in this part of town. After he moved to the Hughes Street address two blocks east, the 1001 N. Garland store was operated by Mrs. Kath Phillips (1939). Green Grocery served customers farther north at 1300 N. Garland (circa 1955) and then Shaddox Grocery occupied a storefront at 1305 N. Garland (circa 1961).

The longest surviving grocery man of John William's children was John Carl Campbell. After his first blush at business at the Rock Street Grocery (223 S. Mill circa 1935), J. C. built his own store at 275 Huntsville. Late in life he reminisced about excavating the basement for his store with a team of mules and an old car hood. J. C. Campbell's Grocery sold a wide array of goods: freshly butchered meats, local produce, tobacco, liquor and beer, and automobile service products including gasoline.

In the same tradition as his father, J. C.'s store was a place that in spite of Sunday liquor laws, a thirsty person with the right nod might find himself able to wet his throat on the Sabbath. J. C. also ran accounts, providing a vitally important credit service to a portion of his clientele in "the holler" who might not otherwise have been able to buy food at all times of the month. J. C. Campbell Grocery remained in continuous operation through World War II when John Carl served in the Navy leaving his wife Opal to oversee a store manager and tend to the care of their six children.

John Carl came to this neighborhood as a competitor to an established grocery concern just three blocks to the east. Finley & Johnson had set up their business at 507 Huntsville Road by 1935. Subsequently, William A. Combs took over grocery sales at this location and Combs Grocery continued at this site until sometime between 1970 and 1975.

In the 1950s, as this part of Fayetteville began to expand, two other groceries appeared on the scene: Ward's Grocery and Service Station at 611 Huntsville Road and Leonard's Food Store at 655 Huntsville. The early 1970's opening of Watson's new supermarket further east proved a difficult competitor (corner of Huntsville and Happy Hollow Road, now demolished).

The old Combs Grocery building and grounds served later years of the 20th century as a location for sales of second hand goods and recycled construction materials.

J. C. Campbell sold his store in 1972. For a few years, it continued as a market under the name of Jim Land's Grocery. After a variety of uses through the 1980s, the property was renovated by its next owners as a water filter sales/service business location.

J. C. Campbell Grocery 1955

Evertt's biggest store, Campbell's Supermarket at 337 S. School, continued after his death under the management of Alton (Alfred) Dewey Morris. The 1962 city directory shows "Campbell's Super Market" in bold type, featuring "Groceries, Meats, Fresh Produce, Open 7 Days A Week." 1969 was the last year for Campbell's Supermarket. In 1972, after the sale of his Huntsville Road store and over fifty years of Campbell business in Fayetteville, John Carl was the last of the line when he retired from the grocery business.

During the later 20th century, grocery markets continued to expand in size and stock variety while shrinking in number. In 1900, Fayetteville's grocers served an average 176 people per store. Patrons were no doubt well acquainted and took time to barter over prices and discuss local gossip and politics. By 1950, the population was 17,071 and served by 37 stores (1 store per 461 people). This trend escalated through the next decades: 1960 population was 20,274 served by 27 stores (1 store per 750 people); 1970 population was 30,729 served by 28 stores (1 store per 1097 people); 1980 census was 36,165, with 27 groceries (1 store per 1339 people); and the 1990 census was 42,099, a population served by 31 stores (including gas and grocery "quick stops") at 1358 people per store.

In 2005, only eight major grocery stores served a Fayetteville population of 58,047 (1 store per 7256 people), assisted by a sprinkling of quick-stop markets and specialty groceries such as Ozark Natural Foods and ethnic food markets. In the downtown area, only the IGA Superstore remains (380 N. College) and is challenged steadily by customers who increasingly shop at the all-in-one retail outlets of Wal-Mart. To the east, Harp's and a neighborhood Wal-Mart provide groceries and more for households along Mission (Highway 45), Crossover Road (Highway 265), and old Huntsville Road (Highway 16 East).

To the north, a Harp's Grocery holds on at Fiesta Square (intersection of North College and Rolling Hills Drive) competing with another Wal-Mart operation at the Northwest Arkansas Mall. Serving the University, the North Garland Harp's functions as a neighborhood grocer. To the west, Wal-Mart's expansion to include groceries at their Highway 62 (West Sixth Street) store resulted in the closing of the Westgate IGA around 2001. Only in south Fayetteville does the Southgate IGA remain the primary grocery operation at its location on the corner of South School and 15th Street.

Grocery sales today is a complex of advanced packaging technology, transportation networks, global markets, and high-volume competition. Corporations have taken over from individual proprietors to maintain ownership, decide management and employment, and manipulate stock and pricing for maximum profit. No longer a hands-on enterprise of personal grit and trading savvy, the piquant grocery business of early America—the business John William Campbell knew and taught his children—is a thing of the past. Flavorful remnants remain, however, preserved in open-air farmers' markets offering homegrown produce and curbside vendors who sell watermelons from the backs of their pickup trucks.

Appendix I: Wagon Production in Fayetteville

The 1st edition (1884-5) of The Arkansas State Gazetteer & Business Directory (Atlanta: R. L. Polk & Co.) named Henry Sweitzer as Fayetteville's wagon maker and blacksmith. He is followed by D. B. Jobe, listed as wagon maker in the 2nd edition (1888-9). Sweitzer Wagon Company is listed in the 3rd edition (1892-3), established in 1887 by E. B. Harrison and Ellis Duncan with officers named in the 1892 directory as Clifford Boles, president; Mac Devin, treasurer, and Ellis Duncan, secretary and manager. In 1896, Ozark Wagon Company was established with Erastus Pitkin as president and Samuel Sandford and Ellis Duncan as partners.

According to Campbell's history, Clifford Boles bought into Ozark Wagon and embarked on an expansive promotional effort which included raffling off "the most elaborately finished wagon the city had ever seen" on the downtown square in 1897. Ozark Wagon Company facilities sprawled over the hillside north of West Center between the railroad and Evergreen Cemetery and included a spur track that ran into the center of the complex. Their models ranged in price from $55 up to $75. The tools of their manufacture included "a boiler, engine, band saw, shaper, planer, jointer, sander, rip saw, 'tenanter,' hollow auger, boring machine, punch threader, tire bender, and miscellaneous blacksmith tools, including punchers, shears, tire cooler, blower and anvil."[1]

The 4th edition of the Arkansas Polk directory (1898-9) names Edward Bumpass as wagonmaker, Daniel Jobe wagon maker, Rush P. Nifong wagonmaker, and Wm. J. Sanders wagonmaker. Also listed was Poore & Rowell Wagon Yard (W. B. Poore and G.

---

[1] Foldvary, Ron "Ozark's $55 Wagon," *Flashback*, May 1980 p 16-17 WCHS. Mr. Foldvary notes that the word "tenanter" probably referred to the tenon saw, a thin-bladed saw used by wheelwrights.

W. Rowell). The 5th edition (1906-7), superseded by the first Fayetteville Polk Directory published in 1904, named Edward Henno as general blacksmith and wagonmaker, Daniel Jobe wagonmaker, and Fayetteville Wagon, Wood, and Lumber Company (J. H. Berry president, W. C. Swift, sec'y and treasurer).

The 1904 Fayetteville City Directory notes in its description of local industry that "The famous Ozark Wagon is made here – an honestly constructed wagon especially adapted for use in surrounding country, a supreme test which readily appeals to the wagon buyer everywhere. The capacity of the plant is tested in meeting an increased demand for a good wagon." Corporate records for 1907 show Duncan as the majority partner with 300 shares ($7500), E. Pitkin with 100 ($2500), E. C. Boles with 60 ($1500), and C. P. Boles with 120 ($3000). 1908 records show Duncan out and E. P. Boles still in with over 300 shares.

Washington County Chancery Court file #306 chronicles legal proceedings for Ozark Wagon Company in 1909, in which Fayetteville Building and Loan Association foreclosed on a $2800 loan taken out in Sept 1902. Payment had not been made in over six months. In the company's 1908 financial statement, assets included real estate valued at $9600, machinery and tools valued at $2500, personal property valued at $13,100, merchandise on hand valued at $9095, and accounts receivable at $3939. Debt totaled $12,650, including a loan balance of $2487.66.

By 1920, no wagon makers remained in Fayetteville, although G. D. Logan's wagon yard remained in operation at 38 East Mountain. This enterprise still existed in 1927 as Fayetteville Wagon Yard, 34 East Mountain. Sligo Wagon Wood Company with offices at 1 McIlroy Building was listed under "Wagon" in the 1929-30 city directory, but by 1932 there were no listings for "Wagon" to be found.

Appendix II: Sligo

In the development of the United States iron industry, the Irish and the name "Sligo" were often connected. The word "Sligo" is Irish, from *Sligeach* meaning "the place of shells." Sligo is the name of the seaport town as well as the name of the county in the province of Connacht, Ireland, situated on Sligo Bay and the Garvogue River (originally Sligo River) 111 miles northwest of Dublin in farming country. The port served surrounding landlocked counties, most notably County Leitrim where rich deposits of iron ore had supported an ancient mining and smelting industry among the oldest in Ireland believed introduced by Celtic invaders around 600 BCE.[33] An early Christian period (5th - 7th centuries) iron smelt appears in the central court of the Creevykeel Court Cairn in County Leitrim, just one example of what was no doubt a proliferation of clan enterprise in this technology. Centered in the Lake Allen area of County Leitrim, charcoal-fired iron smelters powered a tremendous industrial growth in Ireland, with the bulk of its product shipped out through Sligo.

By the mid-18th century, Leitrim's rich iron deposits were temporarily abandoned because the forests had all been cut and there was no longer any fuel to fire the furnaces. Later, coal deposits were found and the industry revived. But at the time, men skilled at these trades began to seek new territories.

Simultaneously, increasing political and religious pressures in Ireland added impetus to the search for new homelands, and land was readily available in the American colonies. By 1634, the Church of England under King James I had persecuted protestant believers in Scotland, driving them to Ireland where they founded

---

[33] http.//www.mhti.com/mines_in_ireland_files/creevelea.htm

the Presbyterian church. Continuing persecution there led to their removal to America between 1728 and 1730.[34]

Among the first waves of Scots-Irish Protestant immigrants were many who worked in the iron industries of the American colonies. Men of means were among the first to seek greater fortune, and those from Ireland experienced in the iron business knew what configurations of land to look for in searching out new deposits of ore. And they knew how to build good furnaces. Of particular application in naming their American enterprise was the word "Sligo," both as a reminder of their recent homeland and of a place that had been connected with the iron trade.

Irishmen founded the Great Sligo Iron Works at Pittsburgh, a firm first named Barnett, Shorb, & Co. circa 1820. Pennsylvania forges where raw ore was smelted included the Sligo Iron Works ca. 1800–1860 in Huntingdon Co. and the Sligo Rolling Mill in Allegheny County ca. 1825-1837, with later production at Sligo Iron Mills in Allegheny County ca. 1845 and Sligo Iron and Steel Company in Fayette County ca. 1870. The Sligo Furnace and Iron Works, located on Licking Creek, Village of Sligo, Piney Township, Clarion County, Pennsylvania, was built in 1845, with a capacity of 1560 tons. Its owners were listed as Lyon, Shorb, & Company: William Lyon of Pittsburgh, J. P. Lyon of Sligo, Anthony Shorb and Thomas McCulloch of Sligo.

"The furnace received its name from Sligo, near Pittsburgh, where the company's iron works were situated; changed to hot blast in 1857; employed chills; produced in 1845 1500 tones; in 1856, 2400 tones of rolling-mill iron. ...The Sligo and Madison Company was the only one to introduce "chills" (iron molds). All the other furnaces ran their metal into sand." It used argillaceous carbonate

---

[34] http://freepages.genealogy.rootsweb.com/~jessebarnett/chucktod.htm

ore to make a "close gray iron," and employed 75 men and boys, with 40 horses and mules.[35] The Pennsylvania mills employed Irish workers such as George White, "a Scotch Irish native of Ireland and an iron roller in the Sligo Iron Works at Pittsburg.[36] John Lyon himself was several generations removed from Ireland. He served as senior member of the Lyon, Shorb & Co. enterprise, which reportedly owned and operated Pennsylvania and Bald Eagle furnaces, Tyrone and Coleraine forges, Sligo iron works, and several large rolling mills in Pittsburg. Born 1784 in Pennsylvania, he was a Presbyterian.

From Pennsylvania, iron-working Scots-Irish moved westward, exploring the frontier for natural resources that might make them rich and offer opportunity to other Irish immigrants. For example, Alexander L. Crawford, born near Norristown, Montgomery County, Pennsylvania, on February 5, 1815, "came of old Irish stock, his paternal great-grandfather having migrated to this country from Ireland about the year 1720." While the occupations of his grandfathers are not known, at the age of 27, Alexander began his career in iron. He "purchased the Springfield [PA] furnace and made charcoal iron for the use of the rolling mill and in 1847 he built the Tremont blast furnace, near New Wilmington, Lawrence County, PA, which he sold out ten years later. ...In 1876 he built the Sligo furnaces in Dent County, Missouri, which are still in operation, making fifty tons of charcoal iron daily."[37] The historical narrative continues to describe Mr. Crawford's development of coke furnaces, coal mines, and railroading.

---

[35] http://paironworks/rootsweb.com/clasligo.html
[36] www.premiernet.net/~ccarley/francis%20ann%20letter.htm
[37] from *Encyclopedia of Contemporary Biography of Pennsylvania*, Vol. II, 1868, as noted at
www.rootsweb.com/~pamercer/PA/Biographies/bioAlexCrawford.htm

Among other positions, he is listed as the Vice-President of the Sligo Furnace Company of Missouri. His second son, Hugh A. Crawford, is described as "engaged in the iron business in St. Louis and is vice-president of the Continental Bank of that city." [38]

"Sligo" became the name of several iron works and communities as industry moved west. Sligo Iron Forge in Marshall County, Indiana was established in 1845 by Charles Crocker, who left for the California gold rush in 1850 to become a wealthy merchant in Sacramento, elected to the state legislature, and a founder of the Central Pacific Railroad helping to supervise its construction across the Sierra Nevada mountains.[39] Alexander Crawford and other founders of Sligo Furnace in Dent County, Missouri tapped veins of iron and lead and harvested virgin forest "to make

---

[38] Mr. Crawford's first son, Andrew, ventured north to Indiana where he is credited as "the Terre Haute capitalist primarily responsible for transforming Vigo County into a national iron and steel center. Founded by Alexander and Andrew, the Vigo Iron Company centered first on a large blast furnace then four years later a rolling mill known as Wabash Iron Company later to be named The Terre Haute Nail Works. Andrew assumed management of the Terre Haute mills in 1880, at which time "the blast furnace employed 300 people and produced 15,000 tons of pig iron, mill iron, and Bessemer steel annually. Before Alexander's death in 1890, the assets of the Nail Works were transferred to Terre Haute Iron & Steel, a stock company with 500 employees producing 600 kegs of nails daily. ... When dwindling Great Lakes ore deposits and cheaper Southern labor impaired the local smelting business, Crawford built an ironworks in Gadsden, Tenn., but kept local mills functioning. In 1899, as his health began to fail, he sold the two mills to Republic Steel. Both mills were closed in 1901." Andrew was also believed president of the Sligo Iron and Steel Company of St. Louis but is not listed among its board of directors in the 1900 Articles of Incorporation. See www.indstate.edu/community/vchs.wvp/!crawfor.pdf
[39] www.indianahistory.org/library/manuscripts/collection_guides/BV0085.html

charcoal used to fire the furnaces which extracted the iron.[40] It was operational until 1921. Irishmen not from County Sligo still used that name for iron working ventures, trading on its increasingly familiar association with that enterprise.

The book *Making Iron on the Bald Eagle,* by Gerald Eggert tells the story of Irish immigrant Ronald Curtin who in 1810 "launched a charcoal ironmaking operation in central Pennsylvania that continued for 110 years."[41] The family history of Hon. William Wirt Culbertson, born 1835 in Mifflin County Pennsylvania and descended of Presbyterian Scots, became "attached to furnace life" and spent his early career at Ohio furnaces and later at Kentucky furnaces, establishing the Ashland Foundry Company. In Wisconsin, Michael Crotty, a pioneer of Adams in Green County, had been born in Sligo Ireland in 1819 and after immigrating to America in 1842 "engaged in mining at various locations until 1846, then removed to his farm and devoted his time thereafter to farming."[42]

At least eleven states host current or past settlements named Sligo: Colorado, Kentucky, Louisiana, Maryland, Mississippi, Tennessee, and Texas, with five known to have been established around a mining/furnace operation in Indiana, Missouri, Ohio, Pennsylvania, and Wisconsin. Businesses and rail lines formed as off-shoots of the Sligo/iron relationship. Bixby, Missouri hosts a railroad station for the Sligo and Eastern line. Sligo No. 18, a potbelly heating stove with a top rack for three irons, made of cast iron and measuring 48-inches, is currently listed among other antiques and "collectibles" in an online price guide. The North Texas Blacksmiths Association includes a Sligo anvil in its roster of

---

[40] www/viburnum.net/History/history/html
[41] Keystone Books 1999
[42] www.monticellowi.com/GreenCo/AdamsHistory.htm

historical pieces.[43] A description of the 1857 town square of "Old Jacksonville" Illinois included a hardware store whose sign stated "Sligo Iron and Hardware."[44]

The Iron Rolling Mill (Eisenwalzwerk), 1870s, by Adolph Menzel
Original work in color, Wikipedia

---

[43] www.blackiron.us/anvils.html
[44] www.rootsweb.com/~ilmaga/newspapers/square.html

Appendix III: The Phipps/Fulbright Mill and Arkansas Forests

The longest lived of Fayetteville's mills—although not located at Fayette Junction nor as far as can be determined was it originally dedicated to producing wagon parts—was that of J. H. Phipps, who had established his milling operations in 1898. Phipps Lumber Company occupied a prominent location on the west side of old Fayetteville on the original Prairie Grove Road, now the site of a Chick-fil-A, Sonic fast-food drive-in, and Arby's at the southeast corner of 6th Street and Razorback Road.

By 1915, Mr. Phipps saw the coming decline of timber harvest along the established railways. Thirty-five years of frenzied sawing had cleared the hillsides within reasonable distance from the rail lines. Not willing to stand by and watch the decline of his profitable enterprise, he began developing a plan to reach the vast forests southeast into Franklin County. He bought thousands of acres of forest land in Madison and Franklin counties. He brought together Ed. E. Jeter of Combs, Jesse Phipps of St. Paul, and J. M. Williams and W. J. Reynolds of Fayetteville as partners in the formation of the Black Mountain and Eastern Railroad. They built a line that joined the St. Paul track at Combs and plunged south into the mountains.

According to Clifton Hull's *Shortline Railways of Arkansas*, "There were trestles which spanned gulches 125 feet deep. At the Cass end of the line, the grade was so steep the locomotive couldn't pull a car of logs up the mountain, so the cars were snaked to the summit one at a time by a team of oxen. In May 1916, the name was changed from the Black Mountain and Eastern to the Combs,

Cass, and Eastern. It was abandoned in 1924."[45]

Another short-term tangent for hauling logs sprang from the Pettigrew terminus, a tram line called the "spoke plant tram." Railroad historian Tom Duggan notes that this line ran from the Little Mulberry River to a point several miles south of Pettigrew called Campground.[46]

Phipps sold out to Jay Fulbright in 1920, and by the time of the plant's demolition in the 1980s, it was commonly known as the Fulbright mill. As late as the 1970s, local residents could visit the mill where an accommodating workman in overalls would deftly replace the hardwood handle of the hoe, shovel, rake, or other metal implement in question.

In 1928, the plant was reportedly the "biggest plant of its kind west of the Mississippi."[47] During World War II, Phipps Lumber Company under the guidance of Bill Fulbright bought out Springfield Wagon Company and brought with it to Fayetteville "over a dozen new families...a sizeable payroll and...a market for more Arkansas timber."[48]

Timber remains an important industry in Arkansas. Evidence of individual logging operations on private and public lands can be found in Pettigrew, where stacks of logs awaiting transport accumulate in the same place where the old railroad roundhouse was located. The hardwood forests of the Arkansas Ozarks have been the focus of nearly fifty years of conflict between forest industry participants and conservationists who want public forests

---

[45] Hull
[46] Personal communication to the author, postcard dated February 2004.
[47] Campbell p 39
[48] *Northwest Arkansas Times* undated clip, front page; Box 20, file 13 WCHS vertical files, UA Special Collections

protected from indiscriminate and harmful harvesting techniques such as clear cutting. Wildlife habitat, watershed protection, and recreational uses have become equally as important as the benefits of timber harvest.

In other parts of the state, timber production is largely a corporate enterprise involving pine "plantations" where mature pine crops are mechanically harvested, hybrid seedlings are planted, and native vegetation is "suppressed" by use of herbicides.

In 1997 the Arkansas Educational Television Network produced "Out of the Woods," a documentary that "takes an in-depth look at Arkansas' timber industry."

> The program shows that farming, the railroad industry, and a boom in logging have forever changed Arkansas' forests. Through forestry research, careful land management and restoration efforts, however, new forests in the Natural State are thriving. In a study of forested land in the state from 1988 to 1995, each region showed an increase in the number of acres reforested.

Conservationists would argue the term "reforested," pointing out that a monoculture of fast-growing pine has been established where mixed hardwood forest had grown.

The thirty-minute AETN video "demonstrates that harvesting timber is the state's biggest industry. Giant paper mills, plywood plants and saw mills pump $1.4 billion dollars into Arkansas' economy ever year. Fifteen percent of the entire Arkansas work force is employed in the timber industry. The industry provides 40,000 jobs and an annual payroll of $938 million. In southern Arkansas, the business of harvesting trees has given birth – and continues to sustain – small towns throughout the pine belt."[49]

As a result of the massive clear cuts and the environmental degradation wrought by the timber boom period and/or the extreme topography of some areas, the government ended up owner of thousands of acres of cut-over, nonproductive land. This is particularly true in the rugged landscape of south and southeastern Washington County, southern Madison County, and northern Franklin County, which became the western part of the Ozark National Forest.

A poem preserved at Shiloh Museum provides a slice of life from the Phipps Lumber Mill operation:

Who's Who and What They Do At Phipps

There's a hard-wood plant near our city
An industry of highest rank
Manufacturing buggy, plow and wagon stock
And all kinds of hardwood plank.

Lee Moore is our good superintendent
And he's always on the hop
For to manage a business like this is
Takes a man that knows no stop.

Bill Swaney is the master mechanic
He's built many mills here and there
He studies and schemes and sets up machines
And keeps them in good repair.

Emmet W. Lucas
Is foreman of the shop
He don't get around like a whirlwind
Yet he knows what his men are about.

Sam Swaney is the engineer
He keeps the engine running good

---

[49] See www.aetn.org/OOTW/

And when he pulls the big whistle
She roars like a bull in the woods.

Jim Dixon runs the jointer
And also the ripsaw too
And with his helper daddy Dodd
They put the timber through.

Frank Osburn runs the bandsaw
At this Frank has no match
It makes no difference what the pattern may be
For he saws it to the scratch.

At the plainer is Billie Winkle
Dressing timber all the day
While his helper daddie Bogan
Is trucking it away.

Mose Osburn runs the shaper
With arms like the legs of a mule
If its light or heavy it matters not
Mose shapes it good and true.

And when they start the big tongue machine
Oh you ought to hear her hum
But when it comes to keeping steam
Well, the fireman most has to run.

It makes both the tongues and double-trees
And finishes them up just right
And whether you work at the front or the rear
You've got to go in "high."

Harvey, Crossno, Graham, and Harper
At the turning lay this they work
Turning yokes and spokes and singletrees
And have no time to shirk.

Sang Brothers are the sanders
And theirs is no easy task
They sand all day on yokes and spokes
But they finish them smooth as glass.

Shorty Smith and Edward Bogan
In the finish shed you'll find
Grading spokes and felloes
And tieing them up with twine.

The work on the yard sometimes is hard
And sometimes it's easy too
But if you haven't some sand in your craw
Toating tongues won't appeal to you.

Claud Guist is the loading boss on the yard
He loads the cars to their brims
Sometimes axles sometimes tongues
And sometimes hickory rims.

Or it may be felloes or wagon spokes
And a lot of singletrees too
And this is the motto of this plant
"Direct from the stump to you."

Bob Hannah is foreman of the bending plant
Where they bend plow handles and rims
Vernon Swaney is the engineer
John Grissom keeps the steam.

Add Baker runs the big bender
Bending rims and wagon hawns
Etter Hannah does the "nailing out"
Chas. Minn does the "knocking down."

Taylor Jordan runs the moulder
Dressing handles all to size
Geo Moore and Guage do the bending
And stack them away to dry.

I am the company's wood-hauler
I've hauled wood this city o'er
And when I drive up to a woodshed
There's always a smile at the door.

For the wood is sound oak and hickory

With sometimes some ash and gum
And the housewife knows as she fills up her stove
Her cooking will soon be done.

And then when Tuesday rolls around
We all look for "Uncle Jay"
For he's the man who has the stamps
And we always get our pay.

So we're a jolly good bunch of "hardwooders"
Earning bread as best we know how
For it was spoken in the garden of Eden
Thou shalt live by the sweat of thy brow.

by B. W. Sivage
(Woodhauler)

Made in the USA
Las Vegas, NV
02 April 2024